Crossing Over to Canaan

Gloria Ladson-Billings

Crossing Over to Canaan

The Journey of New Teachers in Diverse Classrooms

JOSSEY-BASS
A Wiley Company
San Francisco

Jossey-Bass books and products are available through most bookstores. To contact Jossey-Bass directly, call (888) 378-2537, fax to (800) 605-2665, or visit our website at www.josseybass.com.

Substantial discounts on bulk quantities of Jossey-Bass books are available to corporations, professional associations, and other organizations. For details and discount information, contact the special sales department at Jossey-Bass.

Manufactured in the United States of America on Lyons Falls Turin Book. This paper is acid-free and 100 percent totally chlorine-free.

Library of Congress Cataloging-in-Publication Data

Ladson-Billings, Gloria.
  Crossing over to Canaan : The journey of new teachers in diverse classrooms / Gloria Ladson-Billings.— 1st ed.
      p. cm. — (The Jossey-Bass education series)
  Includes bibliographical references (p.) and index.
  ISBN 0-7879-5001-7
  1. Afro-American students—Education—Case studies. 2. First-year teachers—Training of—United States—Case studies. I. Title. II. Series.
  LC2717 .L32 2001
  371.829'96073—dc21   00-011965

FIRST EDITION
HB *Printing*   10 9 8 7 6 5 4 3 2 1

The Jossey-Bass Education Series

Contents

For Jessica,
for whom Canaan is a real possibility

Preface

As was true for many African Americans, an important part of my education took place in the black church. Every Sunday morning meant putting on my best clothes, getting a special hairdo, and spending almost four hours at White Rock Baptist Church in West Philadelphia. We always went to Sunday School at 9:30 A.M. and to Sunday morning services from 11:00 A.M. to 1:00 P.M. I do not think I was alone in experiencing a weird combination of boredom and fascination with the weekly going-to-church ritual.

Depending on the quality of one's Sunday School teacher, it was possible to learn quite a bit about the mystery of faith, even if it was difficult to understand the homiletic proclamations of the preacher. Sunday School teachers often told Bible stories in ways that made sense to children and young people. One of the stories that always puzzled me was that of Moses and the exodus of the children of Israel from Egypt.

I understood the miraculous burning bush, the various plagues that were visited upon Egypt, and the parting of the Red Sea. Indeed, Cecil B. DeMille helped me to see and understand them. What I could not understand was why, after all he had done to whip the children of Israel into shape, Moses was being denied the opportunity to lead them into Canaan. Instead, the younger, less-experienced Joshua was chosen to direct the crossing into Canaan. Why couldn't Moses go into the promised land?

Crossing Over to Canaan: The Metaphor

I probably do not have enough theological knowledge to understand the subtleties of biblical exegesis. But I do know how to recognize a good metaphor when I see one. The passing of leadership from the old to the young is what those Bible stories—and what *Crossing Over to Canaan*—is all about.

We are in the midst of spirited discussions in this country about teachers and their preparation. There are reasons to be pessimistic about the future of our schools. In the midst of this information age, fewer and fewer of our best and brightest students choose teaching as a career. Of those who do, only a small percentage want to teach in urban communities serving poor children of color.

This book is about that small number of prospective teachers who *want* to teach poor children of color. It is about a group of modern-day Joshuas who are excited about the possibilities for transformation that lie just beneath the surface of most urban communities.

As I did in my previous book, *The Dreamkeepers,* I have written this one in three voices—the voice of a teacher, a teacher educator, and a researcher. I reflect on my own early teaching career and the many mistakes I made. I reflect on my work with prospective teachers struggling to work effectively with diverse groups of students. And I attempt to systematically study the practice of novice teachers who are committed to principles of equity and social justice and high achievement for all students.

In this book I describe how prospective teachers who attempt to develop a culturally relevant pedagogy negotiate their first year. But the book is not about personalities. It is about a process—a process of change that can happen in a teacher education program.

Contents of the Book

Crossing Over to Canaan begins with an Introduction that describes my perspective on the state of teacher education in the United States. As one might imagine, my description is not particularly flattering. I explain what I see as a persistent resistance to change in teacher education that keeps the field in a reactive mode. Rather than innovate, teacher education tends to imitate. The book tells part of the story of an innovative teacher education program we call Teach for Diversity (TFD).

Chapter One focuses on the nature of teaching in the twenty-first century and the despair people seem to feel about trying to teach "these children." In this chapter I reveal my inspiration for deciding to focus on novice teachers as a part of the solution to invigorating teaching and supporting success in urban schools.

Chapter Two introduces the novice teachers who agreed to participate in this study. As I stated, I did not attempt to focus on the teachers in great detail, lest the reader become seduced by their individual personality traits. I attempted instead to tell a bit about the teachers' backgrounds and how they came to make the decision to participate in a teacher education program focused on diversity, equity, and social justice.

Chapter Three describes the first of three propositions that support culturally relevant teaching—academic achievement. In this chapter I describe how the novice teachers attempted to take up the academic responsibilities of teaching. They were all bright, knowledgeable young women who wanted to do stimulating, creative things in the classroom. However, their foremost concern was whether or not students were learning, not whether they were being entertained.

Chapter Four addresses the concept of cultural competence. The novice teachers understood that students of color may become alienated from the schooling process because schooling often asks children to be something or someone other than who they really are. It asks them to use language other than the one they come to school with. It asks them to dismiss their community and cultural knowledge. It erases things that the students hold dear. The novice teachers were attempting to recruit the students' cultural knowledge as a vehicle for learning, as well as for understanding how their own cultural background provide a very specific lens for seeing the world.

Chapter Five explores the citizenship function of teaching in public schools. It describes aspects of the community service portion of the teacher education program, as well as the novice teachers' attempts at integrating social justice and civic participation activities into their curriculum.

Chapter Six analyzes some of the shortcomings of the TFD program and creates a vision of a teacher education program that I compare to a promised land. This vision is culled from elements of a variety of teacher education programs I have observed or read about. The chapter offers some cautionary notes to teacher educators about the difficulty of maintaining the effort to innovate in teacher education. However, I trust that it does not act as a deterrent to energetic and creative colleagues who are committed to a transformative agenda for teaching and teacher education.

I have included two appendixes at the end of the book. One describes the methodology employed in the study; the other provides a more detailed description of the TFD program. I include them because I invite teachers, teacher educators, administrators, and qualitative researchers to participate in similar research and practice activities. Ultimately, I want us all to find a way to cross over to Canaan.

Acknowledgments

I have not yet figured out how to do research by myself. Once again I must acknowledge the students, teachers, colleagues, friends, and family who made this effort possible. First, I want to thank the prospective teachers who were willing to allow me to make public their thoughts and actions as a way to help others understand the struggles of new teachers. I am forever in their debt.

Second, I thank those colleagues who were co-laborers in our effort to develop a teacher education program that directly confronted issues of diversity and difference. Chief among them are Mary Louise Gomez, Ken Zeichner, Tom Popkewitz, Mimi Bloch, Carl Grant, Beth Graue, Pat Enciso, Linda Stanley, Jim Stewart, and Mariamne Whatley. At one time or another I came crying to their doors for support and guidance throughout this project.

Third, I must thank the "underground railroad" of scholars who challenge my thinking and ensure that I uphold the high standards of those who have come before—those who traveled up the "rough side of the mountain." I offer specific thanks to Joyce King, Mwalimu Shujaa, Jacqueline Irvine, and Carol Lee.

Finally, I must acknowledge the love and support of my family. Projects such as these translate into many missed dinners, school performances, and sporting events—the glue that holds many families together. My husband, Charles, and daughter,

Jessica, carried on the business of being a family when I was busy spending time with a tape recorder, piles of notes, and the computer.

With this amount of love and support it would seem that this should be a perfect book. I am sure that it is not. However, the mistakes are mine alone and cannot be attributed to any of those who have helped me.

Madison, Wisconsin   Gloria Ladson-Billings
February 2001

The Author

Gloria Ladson-Billings is a professor in the Department of Curriculum and Instruction at the University of Wisconsin-Madison and a senior fellow in urban education at the Annenberg Institute for School Reform at Brown University. Her research interests concern the relationship between culture and schooling, particularly successful teaching and learning for African American students. Her publications include *Dreamkeepers: Successful Teachers of African American Children* (San Francisco: Jossey-Bass, 1994), the *Dictionary of Multicultural Education*, with Carl A. Grant (Phoenix: Oryx Press, 1997), and numerous journal articles and book chapters. She is currently the editor of the Teaching, Learning and Human Development section of the *American Educational Research Journal* and a member of several editorial boards, including *Urban Education*, *Educational Policy*, and *The Journal of Negro Education*. She currently serves as member-at-large on the American Education Research Association Council.

Ladson-Billings has won numerous awards for her scholarship, including the 1989–90 National Academy of Education Spencer Post Doctoral Fellowship; the Early Career Contribution Award (1995) of the Committee on the Role and Status of Minorities in the American Educational Research Association (AERA); the Multicultural Research Award (1995) from the National Association of Multicultural Education; the

Palmer O. Johnson Award (1996) for an outstanding article appearing in an AERA-sponsored publication; the Mary Ann Raywid Award (1997) from the Society of Professors of Education; and the H. I. Romnes Award (1998) for outstanding research potential from the University of Wisconsin-Madison.

Crossing Over to Canaan

Introduction[1]

I took my first cross-country automobile trip about thirty years ago, heading from Philadelphia to Seattle. My 1968 Volkswagen "bug" was loaded down with most of my worldly possessions. Gasoline cost a mere 35 cents a gallon, so I was ready for an adventure.

The first eight hundred miles of the trip, from Philly to Chicago, were excruciating. The temperature hovered near 90 degrees, and the interstates through Pennsylvania, Ohio, Indiana, and Illinois were toll roads. Everything looked the same, except that on some highways we stopped at intervals to pay tolls. By the time we arrived in Chicago, I was convinced that the trip was a mistake. I wanted to turn around and go back, but a graduate fellowship was awaiting me in the Pacific Northwest.

The next day I resumed my trip, and after driving a few hundred miles through Illinois I reached Wisconsin, where the toll roads ended. Wisconsin, Minnesota, North Dakota, Montana, Idaho, and Washington were open roads. They helped me understand why so much of Americana is caught up in songs of the highways and byways—songs like "Travelin' Man," "Route 66," and "On the Road Again." These songs are about freedom and vision, about starting over and feeling free. This part of the trip showed me a part of America that geography books and encyclopedias fail to capture.

As I pulled into Montana I was taken by a sign that read, "Welcome to Montana. Speed limit 70 at night, drive prudently during the day." Growing up in the hustle and bustle of a big city on the

East Coast, I never imagined that there were places in the country where one could "drive prudently." I floored the pedal of the VW and "prudently" made my way to Washington.

Teacher Education and Road Trips: A Parallel

What does a road trip across country have to do with teacher education? Why talk about open highways in a volume on preparing teachers for teaching diverse groups of children? What does a roadway have to do with teacher certification and programming? I believe I can draw some relevant parallels.

The current situation in teacher education looks a lot like the first eight hundred miles of my trip. The tollbooths are apparent in the myriad of competency tests, content examinations, and performance assessments currently being foisted on teachers and those who would be teachers. The road to teaching is a long, boring highway of sameness, and far too many likely teachers feel the way I did at the end of the first leg of the trip. They want to turn around and go back wherever they came from.

But what if preparing to be a teacher could be more like the second part of my trip? What if prospective teachers could go "70 at night and drive prudently by day?" What if prospective teachers had the opportunity to explore the side roads and the local scenery? What if they had the opportunity to see for themselves those places (and people) they had only read about? What if learning to become a teacher were an adventure of freedom and vision?

Public Agenda produced a report entitled "A Sense of Calling: Who Teaches and Why,"[2] which indicates that most new teachers believe they "could have used far more preparation for the realities and challenges they inevitably had to confront when running real-world classrooms."[3] However, few teacher education programs prepare teachers to be effective in urban classrooms serving diverse groups of students. Haberman[4] argues that the traditional approach to teacher education is counterproductive for teachers in high-poverty, diverse classrooms because it "leads them to perceive a substantial number—even a majority of 'abnormal' children in every classroom."[5]

In a review of the literature on multicultural teacher education,[6] I argue that teacher education has been dominated by a narrative that begins like this: "Public school way back when. . . ." In this narrative we reminisce about some mythical days when all the children were smart and well behaved. In public school way back when (PSWBW) the parents and teachers all agreed about what to do and how to do it. But those wonderful days were interrupted when the "Nine Wise Men" of the U.S. Supreme Court ordered that PSWBW had to desegregate to accommodate "other people's children."[7]

Teacher education's response to the change from PSWBW was to create a new and different set of rules and regulations to add to its current practices. Rather than dismantle the "tried and true" practices, teacher educators believed that adding a course, a workshop, or field experience on diversity would be sufficient to suggest that real change was occurring in the profession.

Now as we enter the twenty-first century, we realize that teacher education continues to languish in the practices of a bygone era. Prospective teachers are likely to be in programs filled with white, middle-class students.[8] These prospective teachers rarely question whether they are being prepared to teach in segregated university settings. And teacher preparation is likely to be directed by white, middle-class professors and instructors. There are almost five hundred thousand full-time, regular, instructional faculty in the nation's colleges and universities;

thirty-five thousand are in the field of education; 88 percent of the full-time education faculty are white; 81 percent of these are between the ages of forty-five and sixty (or older).

The prospective teacher population is also predominantly white. The enrollment of schools, colleges, and departments of education (SCDEs) in the late 1990s was about 495,000. Of these students, 86 percent were white; about 7 percent were African American; about 3 percent were Latino. The number of Asian–Pacific Islander and American Indian–Alaskan Native students enrolled in SCDEs is negligible. Thus while the K–12 student population is becoming increasingly diverse, the prospective teaching population is becoming increasingly monocultural, that is, white, middle class, and monolingual English. And even if SCDEs do begin to offer teacher education programs that include "multicultural" curricula, King[9] argues this way:

> Merely presenting factual information about societal inequity (and human diversity) does not necessarily enable pre-service teachers to examine the beliefs and assumptions that may influence the way they interpret these facts. Moreover, with few exceptions, available multicultural resource materials for teachers presume a value commitment and readiness for multicultural teaching and anti-racist education, which many students may lack initially. (p. 142)

Zimpher and Ashburn[10] contend that "there is little evidence to date that schools, colleges, and departments of education and the programs they maintain are, or can be, a force for freeing students of their parochialism" (p. 44). Instead they argue that teacher education programs must be reconceptualized toward diversity and that reconceptualization must include a global curriculum, an appreciation of diversity, a belief in the value of coop-eration, and a belief in the importance of a caring community.

Similarly, work by feminist teacher educators underscores the problem that our traditional teacher education paradigms have in addressing diversity, equity, and social justice. McWilliam[11] asserts that "in general, the culture of teacher edu-cation has shown itself to be highly resistant to new ways of conceiving knowledge," and "issues of race, class, culture, gender, and ecology will continue to be marginalized while the teacher education curriculum is located in Eurocentric and androcentric knowledges and practices" (p. 61). Further, McWilliam urges a break with the "folkloric discourses of teacher education" (p. 48). This means that teacher education must deal with social justice issues of race, class, and gender—and not just in superficial, vicarious ways. Rather, an important component of preparing to be a teacher is interrogating the way status characteristics like race, class, and gender configure every aspect of our lives.

A New Teaching Context

Susan Moore Johnson[12] points out that the next generation of teachers faces a very different teaching context. For one thing, more career options, particularly for females, are available; women can more easily enter other career paths. For another, beginning teachers may not even see teaching as a life career but as a first career, possibly a first step toward other kinds of jobs such as administrator, curriculum developer, or college-level teacher. A profession outside the field of education might be an ultimate goal.

New teachers are entering the profession at a time when public schooling in particular is under public scrutiny. School choice, vouchers, and charter schools all form a complex constellation of what it means to go to school in this era. Teachers are now faced with high-stakes testing that has consequences for both their students and themselves.[13]

These changed social and political circumstances mean that for teacher education to matter it too will have to change. It will have to offer new teachers a fighting chance to both survive and thrive in schools and classrooms filled with students who are even more dependent on education to make the difference in their life circumstances.

Lack of Change in Education

What is keeping teacher education (and teacher educators) from changing? There are a number of likely factors. First, teacher educators have trouble leading prospective teachers to a place they themselves have not been. New conceptions of difference and diversity mean that new teachers face classrooms and communities not experienced by today's teacher educators.

Teacher educators resist changing teacher education because its current configuration allows them access to the perks and privileges the academy has to offer—status, power (vis à vis classroom teachers and other education practitioners), and autonomy. In a changed teacher education system, educators would work more closely and collaboratively with other teachers and community members.

Teacher educators also resist change because such change is difficult and labor-intensive; most already work very hard. However, they work hard at things that fail to serve the interests of students and families of color or families who live in poverty. They often work hard at reproducing the same kinds of teachers they have for decades. The kind of radical change that we need in teacher education means a reorientation of working relations and values. Such a reorientation may mean that teacher educators will have less time for traditional activities of research and publication—the coin of the realm in most colleges and universities.

Teacher educators may resist change because of fear that their university colleagues will marginalize them even further from the academic mainstream. They may also fear the dissolution of teacher education. The reforms aimed at teaching and teacher education[14] suggest that prospective teachers need to concentrate more on liberal studies (English, mathematics, sciences, social sciences) and less on professional education and certification regulations. If teacher educators advocate for "too much" change, some colleges and universities may see this as an opportunity for severing education from the academy.

Finally, I believe teacher educators resist changing teacher education because there's simply a lot of inertia in the field. We do what we do because it is the way we've always done it. If we have always had a program that requires two years of liberal studies courses, a few foundations courses, a set of methods courses, and a field experience, why change it? Why take the time to analyze what's wrong with a system that we don't think is broken?

Dissatisfaction in the Ranks

But clearly something is broken. The Public Agenda report[15] states that "the new teachers surveyed give their education schools and teacher training programs good overall ratings." But survey questions that ask respondents to provide broad ratings often cloak specific areas of dissatisfaction. Although more than 70 percent of new teachers initially say that their programs did a good or excellent job of preparing them for the classroom, 60 percent believe that most new teachers assume responsibility for classrooms without the necessary experience in managing them. More than half of the new teachers feel their teacher education program focused too much on theory and not enough on the practical aspects of teaching. According to one of the teachers in the Public Agenda report, there is a real disconnect between what happens in the university classroom and what happens in K–12 classrooms: "All these methods classes, Piaget, all that stuff—it's mostly useless."[16]

About 57 percent of new teachers believe that their teacher preparation programs did only a fair or a poor job of preparing them to deal effectively with student discipline. The survey results also indicate that what prospective teachers deem as important is quite different from what educational professional do. Education professionals overwhelmingly urge prospective teachers to create interesting, engaging lessons (and the discipline will take care of itself), whereas new teachers feel compelled to maintain discipline and order in the classroom.

Although most new teachers have positive things to say about teacher education, and they believe it is a necessary part of becoming a teacher, many feel that teacher education needs to be rethought and reconfigured to provide prospective teachers with opportunities to spend more time in classrooms and communities.

The difficulty of changing teacher education does not mean change is impossible. Most people who go into teaching do so because they really want to teach. They enjoy working with students and want to do it despite the lack of financial reward and occupational prestige. But there is a wide gulf between wanting to be a good teacher and actually becoming one. This gulf is particularly large for teachers who opt to teach in schools serving poor students and students of color.

Many of our best veteran teachers are approaching retirement age. What they know and are able to do is likely to be lost to the schools and communities they now serve, which means that our dependence on the ideas and expertise of a new generation of teachers has become greater. Those teachers must be willing to travel new highways and byways of teaching and learning to ensure that all of the children they teach experience academic, cultural, and social success. They are the teachers who will have to "drive prudently" down the roads of education for the new century.

1

Can Anybody Teach These Children?

There's no secret . . . I just deal honestly with
children. They know I don't turn my nose
down at them. . . . If everyone in the neighborhood treated these children with the same
consistent interest, the children would do for
them what they do for me.

—*Marva Collins*

I began teaching early adolescent students in a K–8 school in
South Philadelphia in the late 1960s. Although I was a native
Philadelphian, this part of the city was new to me. When I arrived
about a month after the school year began, my classes were in
chaos. The students were left to a series of substitute teachers and
seemingly decided that school had not officially begun because
their "real" teacher had not shown up. This disorganization was not
surprising to me. I had no fond hopes that the students would be
awaiting my arrival—attentive and prepared to move on in social
studies and English. What was surprising was the "diversity" I experienced in South Philadelphia.

To the casual observer I was teaching predominantly white,
working-class students, along with a number of African American
students who were bused from West Philadelphia. I thought that
myself. But as the year progressed, I learned that I was teaching
white ethnic students—Italian Americans, Irish Americans, Jewish

11

Americans, Polish Americans—of varied religious persuasions—as well as African American students. I also learned that these differences mattered in specific ways, and any success I was to have in the school would be tied to my ability to develop a deeper understanding of the groups to which the children felt an affiliation.

The Teacher Shortage

One of the current concerns plaguing the nation's schools is how to find teachers who are capable of teaching successfully in diverse classrooms. Although teacher education programs throughout the nation purport to offer preparation for meeting the needs of racially, ethnically, culturally, and linguistically diverse students, scholars[1] have documented the fact that these efforts are uneven and unproven.

Several factors interfere with the ability of teacher education programs to prepare teachers for diverse classroom settings. One factor that is rarely discussed in the literature is that most of the teacher education faculty are white. As I said earlier, there are approximately thirty-five thousand education faculty in the United States[2]; 88 percent of the full-time education faculty are white; 81 percent are between the ages of forty-five and sixty (or older). These numbers alone do not prove anything about the ability of the teacher education faculty. However, they may cause us to wonder about the incentive of teacher education programs to ensure that all of its graduates are prepared to teach all students.

One of my former graduate students decided to pursue a teaching credential after completing his master's degree. He chose a credentialing program closer to his home, which was in one of the nation's most diverse states. A month after he began his program, I received a letter from him:

I wish that I could tell you that I have found an outlet for [the] excitement [for learning I experienced in the master's program] here. . . . Unfortunately, my experience here has been quite frustrating. . . .[A]lmost none of the students or faculty hold high expectations for student teachers. It has been depressing to go from reading authors like [Michael] Apple and [Bill] Ayers to studying in a program that constantly reinforces the notion that we are not intellectuals. . . .

At the first meeting with our university supervisor we were told to "watch out for 6th graders. They run around like a bunch of wild Indians." The supervisor . . . also warned us about the evils of middle schools (as opposed to junior highs) and block scheduling. Finally he responded to a student's concern that she would not know her content area well enough by saying, "You're smarter than the students. Don't worry. Besides, if you are stumped you can go on the Internet and get wonderful lesson plans."

During one class we . . . interviewed our university professor. I asked her if she had changed her mind on any major educational issue in the last twenty years and she said, "no." She explained that "The answer is always somewhere in the middle so I don't worry too much about the extreme positions" [personal correspondence, Sept. 2, 1999].

The experience of my former student may not represent all teacher education programs, but one cannot but marvel at the irony of such a program in the midst of a community that comprises students of many racial, ethnic, cultural, and language groups. How is it that teacher education programs can be surrounded by diversity and continue to be oblivious to it?

What *Diversity* Means Today

The diversity that today's new teachers face is qualitatively different from what I faced as a new teacher in the late 1960s. My students were clearly differentiated by their ethnic, cultural, religious, and racial differences during a time when such differences seemed more consequential; today, notions of diversity are broader and more complex. Not only are students likely to be multiracial or multiethnic but they are also likely to be diverse along linguistic, religious, ability, and economic lines that matter in today's schools.

The "success" of the 1960s civil rights movement helped to create an African American middle class with experiences and backgrounds different from their brothers and sisters who remained in the old neighborhoods. Indeed, changes in the economy and political climate created an African American underclass that is less trusting of schools and education. Urban centers began to serve growing numbers of immigrant students from Mexico, Central America, and Southeast Asia. The working-class, ethnic neighborhoods of the 1960s knew nothing of the scourge of drugs like crack cocaine or diseases like AIDS. The industrial economy of the 1960s meant that there was plenty of work for people with high school diplomas and even less education. Homelessness was a condition left to indigent men who struggled with drugs and alcohol, not to families with school children.

Today teachers walk into urban classrooms with children who represent an incredible range of diversity. Not only are students of different races and ethnicities but there are students whose parents are incarcerated or drug-addicted, whose parents have never held a steady job, whose parents are themselves children (at least chronologically), and who are bounced from one foster home to the next. And there are children who have no homes or parents.

In addition to the problems the students experience in their personal lives away from school, the schools create a whole new set of problems for children they deem different.[3] As schools become more wedded to psychological models, students are recruited into new categories of pathology. Students who do not conform to particular behavioral expectations may be labeled "disabled" in some way, that is, suffering from attention deficit disorder, emotional disabilities, or cognitive disabilities. Students do in fact confront real mental and emotional problems, but we need to consider the ways students' racial, ethnic, cultural, linguistic, and socioeconomic characteristics are deployed to make their assignment to these disability categories more likely.

Martin Haberman[4] argues that terms such as *at-risk* become code words for students who are perceived by educators and the public to be "problems" in the schools. And it is no coincidence that status characteristics such as race, class, and linguistic diversity become equated with "at-risk-ness." So prevalent is the language of at-risk-ness that it is not unusual for urban teachers to define their entire class as at-risk. Haberman[5] states:

> The number of children who are perceived as failing or not doing as well as they should be in school is high. It includes 11 percent labeled because of some handicapping condition, and 25 percent more in poverty. To these numbers should be added those that teachers call "gray area" children, who seem to fall between the cracks of the system because they are not diagnosed as needing special help, are not necessarily below the poverty line, do not come from minority backgrounds, and yet do not seem to learn much in school. When these groups are added, their numbers exceed 50 percent in almost every urban school district. This means that urban schools and teachers are defining a majority of their students as children who have problems that exceed the typical classroom teacher's ability to educate them. How is it possible for schools and teachers to define a majority of their clients as people who shouldn't be there, or people they are unable to help?

What *Teaching Well* Means Today

Haberman's question is the crux of the issue. Can anybody teach these children? Who are the teachers capable of transcending the labels and categories to support excellence among all students? Haberman calls them star teachers; I call them dream-keepers. But in both my work and that of Haberman, we have identified experienced teachers who knew how to teach well in challenging circumstances. Teaching well, in this instance, means making sure that students achieve, develop a positive sense of themselves, and develop a commitment to larger social and community concerns. Such teachers are inspiring and admirable, but their ranks are decreasing with each passing school year. The question facing most urban school districts is how to ensure a faculty of effective teachers when there is high teacher turnover and relative inexperience.

By the end of my first week of teaching I was unsure if I wanted to stay in the profession. Some of my concerns were specific to the school I was assigned to. I was one of three African American teachers in the school. One of the other African American teachers was a special education teacher. Most of her students were African American, and the parents of her white students were happy that she was willing to hang in there with them. The other African American teacher was a middle-aged woman who had spent years teaching in a Catholic school. Her Catholic school experience esteemed her in the eyes of a largely Catholic neighborhood. Indeed, almost all of my white students had started out in Catholic school but failed there somewhere between 1st and 6th grade. Mrs. Cromartie was the closest thing to Catholic school our school could expect. I was a new upstart. I had arrived late and it didn't seem like I knew what I was doing. I struggled to get order established, and I was teaching the kids as if I was teaching in a college

class. Predictably, the students did not respond well. They hated
school and so did I. I needed help and wasn't sure where to get it.

New teachers often question whether or not they should be
teaching. In my current work as a teacher educator I often work
to reassure new teachers that it is common for them to feel con-
fused and make mistakes in their early teaching. Most education
professionals forget that no matter what happens during a
teacher preparation program, at the successful completion of
such programs the graduates will be *beginning* teachers. Beginners
need both time and assistance to develop expertise. Too often
beginning teachers are given difficult assignments with limited
professional support.

The National Commission on Teaching and America's
Future[6] details the high degree of teacher turnover among new
teachers. This turnover occurs because beginning teachers are
given the most challenging assignments, with little or no professional support. New teachers are often placed in the schools
serving the poorest students and those who have failed to benefit from schooling, so the students with the greatest educational
needs find themselves being taught by the teachers least prepared to teach them. The beginning teachers experience few
successes, and their own sense of failure drives them from the
classroom. Then more new teachers are hired. The cycle repeats
itself year after year. In Chicago one thousand to fifteen hundred
new teachers are hired each year. In Los Angeles the figure is
closer to five thousand new teachers hired each year. Is it any
wonder that this constant teacher turnover results in school failure for so many students?

After about a month of daily "failure" I decided that I needed to get
some help. I asked Mrs. Cromartie if I could observe in her classroom
during my prep periods. She consented and I got a real (teacher)

education. Mrs. Cromartie prepared more than enough materials and activities for her students. Never mind that she did not "cover" everything; she was prepared. She seemed to anticipate problems and attended to them before they escalated. Mrs. Cromartie knew what she wanted to do every minute of the instructional period. She was not fumbling and looking for things to do. She had a routine. When her students arrived at her classroom there was an assignment awaiting them. Sometimes it was a simple question: "List as many nouns as you see in this classroom" or "Write down everything you have eaten in the last twenty-four hours." The students came in and got right to work. Mrs. Cromartie used this time to take her attendance and get organized. This "pre-class" assignment lasted about five minutes and always served as a lead-in for the day's lesson. Slowly but surely I learned that Mrs. Cromartie was not "smarter" than I. She was "smarter" at managing a class of young adolescents.

The school climate that most new teachers find themselves in does not invite novices to admit shortcomings. Rather, they are encouraged to close their doors and join the ranks of other teachers—isolated and independent from each other. New teachers' lack of expertise about some of the basics of teaching (for example, policies, procedures, routines) places them and the students in their classrooms at a disadvantage. However, we must not assume that inexperience equals incompetence. Indeed, some new teachers demonstrate remarkable skills early in their teaching careers. Such teachers provide us with good models for supporting the professional development of other new teachers as well as experienced teachers.

Case Example: A Model, Novice Teacher

One such excellent novice teacher is a young man I call Carter Forshay.[7] I learned of his story in a summer institute that featured excellent teachers of African American students. Carter was an

African American man in his late twenties. He was excited about his first teaching job. He had completed his undergraduate degree at a university not far from his hometown in the Midwest. After undergraduate school he made his way to the West Coast, an area of the country he longed to see. While there he completed a teacher certification program and accepted a job offer from a large urban school district in California. This job in an exciting, vibrant city seemed a perfect opportunity.

Carter began his first year with the youthful enthusiasm, energy, and idealism of the uninitiated. He made a commitment to ensure that his 3rd graders would demonstrate high levels of literacy. His undergraduate degree was in communications, and in the back of his mind he harbored thoughts of completing a master's degree in the field that might lead to a career in communications. In the meantime Carter saw teaching as a socially responsible career despite its limited financial reward.

Carter's first jolt to reality came when he learned that his students, all African Americans, absolutely hated writing. Several were respectable readers, given that expectations for African American poor and working-class students were exceedingly low. But almost none of Carter's students enjoyed writing. Each time Carter attempted to come up with an exciting and motivating topic on which to write, his students balked. "Aww, Mr. Forshay, I don't want to do this." "Writin' is too hard." "I don't have nothin' to say; why are you makin' us write this stuff?" "Why can't you just give us some worksheets? We can do them!"

Each day these comments and similar ones greeted Carter whenever he proposed a writing task. After several half-hearted attempts on the part of the students and mounting frustration on the part of the teacher, Carter began a systematic examination of his own practice. This is a significant step because he could have chosen to blame the students for their failure. If he had, he would have received plenty of collegial support for this perspective.

Carter began to think about what kinds of things were important in his own life. Chief among them was music. Carter had an extensive collection of vintage and contemporary jazz CDs. He knew that his students also loved music, although their musical taste ran more toward rap and soul. Carter decided to gamble on an idea that helping kids connect with music might be a way to help them connect with writing.

Carter chose a CD by trumpeter Wynton Marsalis that featured a song entitled, "Blue Interlude: The Bittersweet Saga of Sugar Cane and Sweetie Pie." He chose this song because in it Marsalis explains the way he uses the various melodies to reflect particular "characters"—a technique reminiscent of that used in the classical music of "Peter and the Wolf." During the first lesson Carter played the CD and questioned the students about what they thought the action was and how they thought the characters were behaving and feeling. From there, Carter encouraged the students to take turns role-playing the characters and their interactions.

At first Carter's students were reluctant and seemed embarrassed to stand before their peers and play the roles. However, once one of the girls took on the role of Sweetie Pie and two of the boys became Sugar Cane and Cotton Candy, the rest of the students delighted in their actions. After their attempt, Carter urged other triads of students to act out the roles. Each group became more dramatic and more invested in the role play. Carter concluded that day with having the students record character traits of each of the characters.

The next day Carter had the students outline the story and develop some dialogue to accompany the actions of the characters from the previous day. They could use the same words they had heard the day before or create new dialogue. The main thing was for the students to begin to write. They began to discuss various words and phrases, and they prompted each other with comments such as, "No, she wouldn't say that" or "I don't think that makes any sense," or "Now, that sounds good. That's like a *real* story." Each group of students wrote their own version of the story, and their peers served as editors for their drafts. The final drafts included richly detailed stories, with imaginative dialogue and lively illustrations. The students who no one thought would write had become writers.

Using Reflective Practice

How did these students become writers? What did this new teacher *do* that changed their attitudes and encouraged their abilities? It is my contention that Carter decided to work on himself rather than try to "fix" the students. He understood the problem as his, not theirs. He engaged in what teacher educators call reflective practice.[8] This ability to reflect is a learned one. The increasing demands on teachers, both preservice and inservice, require that they spend more and more time trying to get things done rather than thinking about what they have done or what they will do. Reflection is a luxury most teachers do not have the opportunity to indulge in.

Carter's willingness to look at what he was doing also represents a particular outlook or point of view—a view suggesting that the place for improving student performance begins with the teacher. Although it is clear that teachers cannot carry the entire burden for students' academic performance, it should be equally clear that they shoulder some of it. Excellent teachers who are faced with student failure are quick to ask themselves, "What am I doing that contributes to this failure?"

Carter's example is so striking to me because he is a novice teacher. Much of what we know about novice teachers suggests that new teachers frequently lack the insight or presence of mind to employ a reflective practice.[9] Instead, most new teachers are preoccupied with handling the day-to-day challenges of teaching—discipline, classroom management, lesson planning, and implementation. Teachers must make thousands of decisions each day. Rarely do they have the time or inclination to think critically about their decisions. Certainly, some decisions do not require much thought or reflection, for example, whether we should take our outerwear with us to lunch or come back to the classroom between lunch and going outside. However, many seemingly perfunctory decisions should command more thought and attention. We should ask, for example, How many students are being pulled out to attend compensatory programs? How does determining who is receiving hot versus cold lunch represent a social class marker? How arbitrary is the ability grouping in my class?

Learning from Other Novices

Carter's deliberate look at his own teaching practices spurred me to look at the work of other novice teachers. What else might we learn from new professionals that could improve the practice of others, preservice and inservice alike? It is important for us to determine what strengths new teachers bring to classrooms because they are much more likely to be assigned to some of the nation's more challenging teaching circumstances. Once hired, few new teachers in urban schools (serving large numbers of students who are poor, of various racial and ethnic backgrounds, and who speak a first language other than English) receive adequate induction into the profession.[10] Other professions such as medicine, law, and architecture have a well-established system of clinical preparation that supports novices as they grow into greater responsibilities and more complex work.[11]

"Welcome to Meyer School,"[12] the principal remarked. In your social studies class you will be teaching U.S. History, Pennsylvania History, and Philadelphia City Government." That didn't sound too bad. I was solid with the U.S. History and having grown up in Philadelphia, I would be all right with the Pennsylvania History and Philadelphia City Government. "Oh, and since you have an English minor you will be teaching two English classes!" Now, that did sound pretty bad. While it was true that I had enough courses in English to constitute a minor, it was never a subject I had given any thought about teaching.

More distressing than the fact that I would be teaching "out of my area" was the fact that a significant number of my students struggled to read. How was it possible that the principal would allow me—a rookie—to be responsible for teaching poor readers how to read the literature? Wouldn't he get in trouble for allowing this? The next piece of "news" was that since I began the school year late, my "colleagues" had helped themselves to the class sets of history texts. What was left was a hodge-podge of history books—three or four from several different publishers that the school had tried over the years. Was I being inducted into teaching or initiated into a sorority?

Supporting New Teachers

New teachers are among the more vulnerable professionals in schools; they need to be nurtured and supported in the profession. Despite all of their youthful and idealistic enthusiasm, most new teachers are both frightened and overwhelmed by the demands of teaching. They expect (and should receive) well-planned and implemented professional development that helps them learn about their work as they make those first, tentative steps in the profession. They need the opportunity to try new things, and they need to be challenged about preconceived and stereotypical notions that circulate about teaching particular groups of students.

Knowing that new teachers need this kind of support and providing such support are two very different things. However, in an attempt to make a more seamless transition between pre-service and inservice, my colleagues and I[13] developed a program for college graduates who have expressed a desire to teach school in communities serving diverse racial, ethnic, and socioeco-nomic populations. We called the program Teach for Diversity[14] or TFD. We designed TFD as a fifteen-month elementary certi-fication program with a clear mission to prepare teachers to work in diverse learning environments.

We made several assumptions about who might be good can-didates for this program—assumptions grounded in our many collective years of preparing teachers. For example, we knew that many of the undergraduate students who come to teaching come with naïve notions of what it means to teach young chil-dren. We also knew that many of their reasons for wanting to teach came either out of a vague sense of "loving children" or as a part of reduced dreams. Perhaps they started out wanting to be doctors or lawyers but saw those fields as too difficult and now they want to try teaching. We also knew that most of our under-graduate students were very young and that their youth proba-bly constrained the kinds of life experiences they had had. So with TFD, we sought to circumvent the typical selection prob-lems by creating a graduate-level program.

What It Means to Teach

An irony that exists in most schools, colleges, and departments of education is that teaching continues to be relegated to a low status. Even in institutions where there is a Department of Curriculum and Instruction or the more updated version, Department of Teaching and Learning, the emphasis and scholarly effort typically rests with the "curriculum" or "learning" side of the dyad. Issues of instruction or teaching reside mainly in the certification programs under the rubric, "methods." Some of the scholarly work done in "instruction" and "learning" occurs in educational psychology departments, and the substance of this work transcends notions of technical behaviors and strategies that constitute the elements of teaching practice.

Two similar experiences come to mind when I think about pedagogy—one from my own practice and the other from that of Suzanne Wilson.[15] A question I pose to my student teachers in our field experiences seminar is, "What makes you different from any other college-educated person?" Typically, the student teachers struggle to articulate what they know and what they are capable of doing as teachers that is different from the skills, knowledge, and abilities of others. Their struggle reminds me of how poorly we, as teacher educators, have worked to explicate what it means to teach and how bankrupt our theories of pedagogy really are.

Wilson tells the story of her "Introduction to Teaching" course, where some days she taught in a very directive way— standing at the chalkboard, giving information, asking questions. On other days she was more facilitative. She sat among the students, provided them with provocative materials, and allowed them to carry on a discussion. At the end of one of the less-directive, more-facilitative sessions, she asked the students, "Did I teach today?" The students said no, she had not taught. Their notions of pedagogy, probably formed by years of being students, were that teaching occurs when the person designated as "teacher" very deliberately and obviously *controls* classroom discourse. The point of these examples is that even those who have chosen teaching as a profession have naïve and poorly formed notions of what it means to teach.

There are at least two reasons our notions of pedagogy are poorly developed and articulated. One reason we struggle to define *pedagogy* is that the English language uncouples notions of teaching and learning. In a conversation with a Jewish colleague I learned that there is but one word for *teaching and learning* in Hebrew. Thus, a teacher is always a learner, and a learner is always a teacher. However, English has created a dichotomy between teaching and learning that suggests a causal relationship without fully understanding the dynamic that exists between the two. Perhaps this semantic conundrum is best left to the linguists and the philosophers.

The second reason is that naïve and ill-formed notions of pedagogy result from limited theoretical conceptions of pedagogy. In some ways the phrase "theories of pedagogy" seems like an oxymoron. If pedagogy is about practice, how can we conflate it with theory? Schwab[16] describes this dilemma eloquently:

> The incongruity of theory and practice cannot be corrected by a fundamental change in either one or the other. The practical is ineluctably concrete and particular. The strength and value of theory lie in its generality, system, and economy. . . . The very fabric of the practical, on the other hand, consists of the richly endowed and variable particulars from which theory abstracts or idealizes its uniformities. The road we drive on has bends and potholes not included on the map. We teach not literature, but this novel and that. The child with whom we work is both more and less than the percentile ranking, social class, and personality type into which she falls. Yet, we will drive our car smoothly, convey *Billy Budd* effectively, and teach 'Tilda well only as we take account of conditions of each which are not included in the theories which describe them as roads, literature, and learning child.[17]

But I am arguing that if we understand theory to inform practice in other arenas—medicine, law, business, economics— why not consider its implication for informing pedagogical practice? And why not work on more powerful theoretical notions to generate more effective practice? If we claim that, as educators, we operate in a scholarly field, we must be able to explain the way things work in that field. We know that the knowledge we profess may be experimental and "non-explanatory."[18] The theoretical knowledge attempts to explain empirical phenomena, but theories "are more than abbreviated summaries of data, since they not only tell us *what* happens, but *why* it happens as it does."[19] Theory and practice operate in a symbiotic-like relationship. If we are to help novice teachers become good and experienced teachers become better, we need theoretical propositions about pedagogy that help them understand, reflect upon, and improve their pedagogy.

Theories of Pedagogy

Shulman[20] has presented us with a useful rubric for understanding some aspects of pedagogy. His concepts of *content knowledge*, *pedagogical knowledge*, and *pedagogical content knowledge* have formed an explanatory paradigm for teaching expertise.

Content knowledge—what teachers are officially assigned to teach—has occupied much of the space of education. This knowledge purportedly emanates from the "accumulated literature and studies in the content areas and the historical and philosophical scholarship on the nature of knowledge in those fields of study."[21] Thus, cries for reform in teaching often center on what and how much teachers know. Abolishing undergraduate education or diminishing the number of professional education courses, coupled with increased requirements in subject matter courses, are seen as panaceas for poor quality teaching.[22]

Pedagogical knowledge refers to "those broad principles and strategies of classroom management and organization that appear to transcend subject matter."[23] How to organize a lesson plan, explain ideas and concepts clearly, prepare students for a test, group students for instruction, and maintain a sense of order without being autocratic and repressive are examples of pedagogical knowledge that teachers acquire in the preparation and early years of teaching. This general pedagogical knowledge has been the focus of much of the research on teaching.[24]

Finally, *pedagogical content knowledge* refers to the knowledge that is specific to teaching particular subject areas. According to Shulman,[25]

> Within the category of pedagogical content knowledge . . . for the most regularly taught topics in one's subject area, the most useful forms of representations of those ideas, the most powerful analogies, illustrations, examples, explanations, and demonstrations—in a word, ways of representing and formulating the subject that make it comprehensible to others. Pedagogical content knowledge also includes an understanding of what makes the learning of specific topics easy or difficult; the conceptions and preconceptions that students of different ages and backgrounds bring with them to the learning of those most frequently taught topics and lessons.

Grossman suggests that although Shulman's terminology is new, its meaning is akin to Dewey's charge that "teachers must learn to 'psychologize' their subject matter for teaching, to rethink disciplinary topics and concepts to make them more accessible to students."[26]

Notions such as psychologizing teaching are indicative of what Giroux and Simon[27] suggest is wrong with extant theories of pedagogy.

[Their definition of *pedagogy*] refers to a deliberate attempt to influence how and what knowledge and identities are produced within and among particular sets of social relations. It can be understood as a practice through which people are incited to acquire a particular "moral character." As both a political and practical activity, it attempts to influence the occurrence and qualities of experiences. When one practices pedagogy, one acts with the intent of creating experiences that will organize and disorganize a variety of understandings of our natural and social world in particular ways. Such a pedagogy does not at all diminish pedagogy's concern with "What's to be done?" As a complex and extensive term, *pedagogy's* concern includes the integration of practice of particular curriculum content and design, classroom strategies and techniques, and evaluation purposes and methods. All of these aspects of educational practice come together in the realities of what happens in classrooms.[28]

Giroux and Simon argue for a "critical pedagogy that takes into consideration how the symbolic and material transactions of the everyday provide the basis for rethinking how people give meaning and ethical substance to their experiences and voices."[29]

As I understand the work of critical theorists, pedagogy operates in the realm of the relational and societal. No longer are we referring merely to the knowledge transactions that occur in the classroom but to the larger social meanings that are imparted between and among teachers, students, and their social worlds. Critical theorists and pedagogues envision education as a vehicle for human liberation. The content, generic teaching skills, and subject-specific teaching skills are considered a part of a much larger constellation of pedagogical work.

The divergent views of pedagogy—from Shulman to Giroux and Simon—map out the terrain over which educational theorists and teacher educators travel in an attempt to construct meaningful theory and relevant practice. They represent a kind of continuum along which we can construct a vision of pedagogical theory capable of meeting the needs of all students.

Emergence of the TFD Program

In the mid-to-late 1980s colleagues in my department began a series of informal meetings to discuss their growing concerns about the department's elementary teacher education program. Paramount among their concerns was the failure of students to demonstrate a clear understanding and commitment to principles of human diversity, equity, social justice, and the intellectual lives of teachers. One of the concerns expressed by the elementary education students was that they were "tired of having multicultural education shoved down their throats"[30] and felt that everyone [at the university] talked about multicultural education, but "no one showed them how to do it!"

A second concern of the faculty was the continued fragmentation of the academic and professional course work. Students were faced with increasing course requirements, both from the university and the state credentialing agency. However, this loose configuration of courses failed to help students develop a coherent understanding of pedagogy. And taking all of the courses did not seem to help produce a more intellectually disposed person.

The third concern was the disjunction between course work and field experiences that was exacerbated by the typical buyers' market that exists between the university and the local school districts. So overwhelming is the university's need for cooperating teachers that almost any warm body will do, so student teachers may receive very uneven experiences, based on where they student teach and with whom they are placed.

But the overall nature of the discussions in our department was not related to the logistics of credit hours, course sequencing, and student teaching placement. Our conversations over brown-bag lunches were instead an attempt to wrestle with the knotty problems of the underlying philosophical, theoretical, and conceptual tenets on which to construct a new teacher education program. The theoretical lenses through which members of the faculty group viewed their own work ranged from critical to constructivist to postmodern.

The result of these weekly discussions was the TFD elementary certification program, with master's degree—a program designed to prepare teachers to teach effectively in multicultural, social-reconstructionist ways.[31] However, this book is the story of a subcohort of TFD, not a blueprint for building a teacher education program. The book helps us ask how we might think differently about preparing teachers for the challenging work of working with diverse groups of students. It also challenges us to think about what we might learn from novice teachers.

————

My own work with TFD was informed by my previous research with successful teachers of African American students.[32] This work helped me develop a theoretical notion of *culturally relevant pedagogy* that is based on three propositions: *academic achievement*, *cultural competence*, and *sociopolitical consciousness*. In the next chapter I introduce the reader to these terms and begin explaining the complex task of learning to teach.

2

Sojourners

Walk together children, don't you get
weary. . . . There's a great camp meeting in
the Promise Land.

—African American spiritual

After my third year of teaching I decided to go to graduate school
full-time to earn my master's degree. When I returned to Philadelphia, I was assigned to a school located in one of the poorest
neighborhoods in the city. The school was a small annex of mostly
Latino and African American middle school students. Most of my
colleagues were novices. Indeed, my three previous years of teaching placed me in the category of "experienced teacher." But it was
the kind of a place where people were willing to take risks and try
new things. One of my colleagues was a Puerto Rican man who
knew the neighborhood like the back of his hand and used his con-
tacts to bridge the school-community chasm. Another colleague
lived with a starving artist and brought examples of his art in to
stimulate her students' thinking. Still another teacher was married
to a lawyer and invited him in regularly to talk to students about their
legal rights. I decided to teach the students Spanish. This "pedagogical" decision made the Spanish speakers in my classes the
experts—an unexpected position for most of them.

Much of the literature on teacher education attempts to direct prospective teachers to the tried-and-true topics: lesson plans, curriculum design, instructional strategy, and classroom management. School systems debate the merits of various instructional strategies and curricula. Rarely are new teachers encouraged to come up with new ideas and pedagogical innovation. The preparation year typically is one of replication and reproduction. Student teachers often are teaching the exact lessons (or some minor variation) they learned in methods courses. My own daughter has had student teachers in many of her classrooms. In 2nd, 3rd, and 4th grade she had either a student teacher or practicum student; each did a lesson based on what she had learned from her methods course. Unfortunately, each teacher did the *same* lesson! So for three straight years my daughter did the same poetry exercise.

A Community of Teacher-Learners

Despite what we know about the social context of learning, prospective teachers are treated only as individuals who must construct and implement lessons alone. The notion that collective thinking about teaching and learning should be an aspect of preparing to teach is not prevalent in most programs.

Our attempt in Teach for Diversity (TFD) was first to build community among the prospective teachers so that they would be equipped to build community among their own students. Instead of the serendipitous group of teachers I affiliated with in my fourth year of teaching, the cohorts of TFD were deliberately put together to learn with and from each other. In this chapter I introduce one such group of teacher-learners.

The Hughes Cohort

The eight TFD students assigned to the Langston Hughes Elementary School (a pseudonym) were a varied group. All were young women. One was Latina. One was African American. The remaining six were European Americans, but it would be a mistake to assume that the students' racial or ethnic identity labels explained them fully. Throughout the year we learned about the complexity of their lives and their perspectives.

Vanessa

Vanessa was the only African American member of the cohort. At the opening TFD orientation she was visibly upset about the lack of diversity in the group. She had a point. Of the twenty-five members of the group only three were African Americans; two were Latinas. But "lack of diversity" is often about perspective. From our perspective as faculty members at a large, Research 1 university, this was a diverse group. Our typical program was filled with young, white, middle-class, monolingual females from within the state. However, Vanessa looked at the program from an entirely different vantage point. She had just graduated from a historically black college located in a city with a majority African American population. There her classmates were African Americans; most of her teachers were African Americans, and she became confident in her intellectual abilities. Now being plunged into the whiteness of this university made Vanessa think twice about preparing to become a teacher.

> I was like oh, Teach for Diversity, it's going to be a lot of African American and Hispanic people, you know, just a lot of minority people in the program, and the first day I walked

into the room and I was the sole. . . . I mean because Maya wasn't there yet and Jamal wasn't there yet. I was the only African American female in the room and coming from [name of historically black college] and, coming from Atlanta, I said this is not going to work. Maya came in and Jamal came in, and I was like well, you know, and so I went home and I told my mom. I said, "Mom, I can't do this." She said, "Why?" I said, "There are only two other African American people in the program." And she was like, "Well, you didn't go there to entertain with them or you know you're there to *teach* for diversity, to learn how to do this program, and to go through and learn how to teach students of different academic, economic, what-have-you settings and stuff. I thought about it for a while and I was like, well, that's true. So I went back, but it is different because I think I find myself trying to defend African Americans a lot in this program, and I think people hold certain stereotypes, and I have my own stereotypes too. But I just have this feeling that these other people have these stereotypes too just because they were white, and that was my bias.

Vanessa grew up in two distinctly different worlds. She began her life in the South, where she was born. Her mother, a former teacher and current school administrator, moved to the Midwest to pursue professional opportunities when Vanessa was very young. Although Vanessa was very familiar with this predominantly European American community, she could not wait for the opportunity to leave to attend college in a less culturally encapsulated environment.

She chose TFD because it fit her career goals, offered to help defray some of the costs of tuition, and allowed her to live at home. TFD's whiteness was more disappointing than discouraging for Vanessa, but it would not determine her participation or her success. She just had to reacclimate into her former community.

Tara

Tara was a white woman from the local community. She was a graduate of the university and knew the university community well. But something happened during her early adolescence that changed her life and her worldview dramatically.

> I was extremely delinquent in middle school, and . . . and it wasn't that I was with a bad group of friends. I mostly did it alone. I just decided not to go a lot, and I didn't miss anything in the classes. Like I realized that I could . . . I kind of did the bare minimum, and as little as possible to get by was kind of my plan and I think I was just bored. . . .
>
> I read about foreign exchange programs, and we looked into them and we (my parents and I) thought, "This is really expensive". . . . My parents took a student from Japan, and I went to a friend of mine and we traded kids. . . . The first year worked out great except that in the United States you just live in the neighborhood of your school, so he [the exchange student] was really close, but I couldn't just be accepted to any high school in Japan because I didn't take an admission test to get in. So I couldn't go to a high-level Japanese high school because I would mess everything up. So I had to go to a lower-level high school (that was far away from where I was living). It was really hard because I had to take an hour bus ride to school and then back . . . and most of my friends . . . some of them did commute and some didn't, but I didn't get to be around them so I was really lonely my first year.

Tara's experiences in Japan helped her understand the concept of other-ness. She understood what it meant to be considered different and was quickly drawn to the students who seemed to be on the social margins of the classroom.

The biggest lesson that Tara learned while teaching an African American student, "Terrance," was that every now and then she should just leave him alone. Like many young, white prospective teachers, Tara started out believing she needed to "fix" Terrance. "I was truly worried for Terrance [because he felt like I did about school], but I had a great environment [that] kind of put me ahead of the game, but [Terrance] didn't and he's going to struggle in middle school."

But gradually she began to develop another perspective on how she might help Terrance.

> When I finally let go and said, "Well, you're right. It's your life; if this is the way you want it to be, that's fine." And he's like, "You're not going to talk to me?" I said, "Yeah." And then it worked better. I noticed that if I just didn't say anything, that he would eventually come to me and maybe if we'd started that earlier. . . . [My cooperating teacher] and I talked about it a lot at the end of the year, you know, maybe we should have just let Terrance be . . . learn his lines, give us plays once a week on his own, do his thing, do some math tutoring on the side, but basically let him be.

Although this may seem like a minor point, Tara's reflection on how she might better serve Terrance represented a breakthrough. She took her own advice, and before long she began giving Terrance more opportunity to work without a teacher hovering over him. She acknowledged his sense of personhood by allowing him some autonomy. Leaving him alone did not mean that she no longer held him responsible for his work or his action. Instead, it meant that she became more judicious in those things she "decided to notice."

The wisdom to let Terrance alone probably came from Tara's earlier experiences working as an aide with physically abused preteens. She focused on the power differentials that exist between teachers and students and realized that the school as an institution created a barrier between people. It could function to diminish one's sense of personhood. Her strategy with the abused teens was to reconstruct their sense of personhood.

> I wanted to make them comfortable, so sometimes I would take two or three of them to McDonald's, and we'd get to know each other in that setting because the school . . . wasn't a good place to talk one-to-one in a small group.

Tara understood that enhancing students' sense of personhood also allowed her to further develop her own sense of personhood.

> I realized that to be a good teacher you needed to be yourself, and when I tried to play teacher, it didn't work. I wasn't being myself, but when I was myself and told the stories and got them excited about Japan in the unit, and they knew me as who I was, and what my life experience was, [things] worked a lot better.

Robin

Robin reminded me of many of our teacher education students. She was very fair—blond hair, translucent skin, and perky. How she might fit into TFD was the question running through my mind. But as was true of this entire cohort of prospective teachers, there was more to Robin than met the eye.

> I didn't want to go into teaching because I realized how much work is involved in it. I wasn't sure I was ready to commit that much time. So basically, I was a political science undergraduate

and tried a couple of different things before coming to TFD. . . . [I] went to Alaska and lived up there for a year. . . . I learned a lot. I was one of six women originally with a ship of 180 men, so I faced a lot of harassment and different things that I hadn't experienced so vividly before. I also met people from all over the world who had very different ideas and different backgrounds than I did. That was probably where I started to think about my own background in terms of Calvinist ideas and how much they affected my thinking and different morals that I ran into or ideas of what was acceptable or what society expected were very different than what I had grown up with. And it caused me . . . it forced me to reevaluate maybe some of my own ideas.

After her Alaskan experience, Robin went to Puerto Rico. Then she returned to the states and made the decision to consider teaching. But Robin was not impulsive about this decision.

Before I committed to a program, I wanted to make sure that . . . I was good at it or that I had any talent and also that I wanted to devote that much time [to it]. So I became an educational assistant (teacher's aide), which in many ways doesn't require that much time but [I] found myself devoting the extra time anyway. [I was] wanting to make sure that the students were really . . . [that] they had someone who really thought about ways to approach things with them. . . . My position was a "time-out" position and also kind of a tutor but mostly for kids who had difficulty.

Robin grew up in a midwestern, Dutch reform community that was fairly strict in its religious tenets, but during her college years she began thinking critically about her background and the world around her.

I found, even when I was living there in college, when I really was starting to become critical of the culture, I started to think that it was a pretty hypocritical culture . . . supposed to be very religious in its background yet many of the things I saw happening were very much based on . . . greed and keeping money.

Robin's ability to critically analyze her own experience is a skill many teacher educators struggle to engender in white, middle-class, monolingual prospective teachers.[1] Although her community was steeped in a rhetoric of self-improvement and hard work as the antidote to low achievement, Robin was beginning to question such logic.

The Protestant work ethic is very strong there and you can pull yourself up, and I find that at times people don't. . . . They [the community] will never recognize that sometimes that's impossible for people to do.

Brenda

Brenda was also from the Midwest. She grew up in a small resort town and thought of her schooling experiences as pretty typical. Her decision to attend the university was merely following in the footsteps of her three older sisters, all of whom had attended the university before her. However, attending the university did not guarantee her acceptance into its highly competitive teacher education program.

I took the [competency exam] and was like fifth on the waiting list. They said either you could take it again or you could wait. I just thought . . . maybe this is just telling me something. . . . I talked with my adviser and [he] said something about special education, which had really interested me anyway.

Brenda eventually earned both bachelor's and master's degrees in rehabilitation psychology. For five years she worked with adults with disabilities and their parents. A major part of her work was helping to prepare students for jobs and serve as their advocate to potential employers.

> The employers . . . didn't want people with disabilities in there. It was a small town so they saw them anyway, so they saw that "weird guy" walking around and there was no way they wanted *that* person in their employ. So I did a lot of talking and just getting out there and talking with a lot of different people.

Another aspect of Brenda's work was actually doing the work she was training the students to do.

> I was doing a lot of cleaning . . . and I find myself looking at bathrooms like a whole new way. . . . I used to do a lot of office cleaning and bathrooms, and public library cleaning.

Brenda's work with adults with disabilities provided an opportunity for her to see the world from a different perspective. A self-described Goody Two-shoes, Brenda found that just being compliant might be enough to help a white, middle-class woman move along in the educational system, but that did not happen for everyone.

> I think a lot of people saw me as a good student. The teacher saw me as a good student. I think because I was well behaved

and wasn't doing things I shouldn't be . . . and I did pretty good, you know, I had my homework done.

Brenda brought a different perspective to the group by reminding us that students in rural areas and small towns also suffer from stereotypes about what it means to be normal. She pointed out that middle-class people can avoid certain things in cities.

The diverseness in smaller towns, everyone sees that. In bigger towns, people, like those on X Street, they see those people that are looking for money, and they see the same people. But they don't really see them in a grocery store or anything. In a small town, they're everywhere, you know. You see them no matter where you go.

Candy

Candy grew up in a midsized, midwestern town not too different from that of our university. She was the dramatic member of the cohort. She had wanted to be an actress and studied drama in college. She saw acting as a much-needed relief from her Catholic school upbringing.

I went to Catholic schools for twelve years . . . and I had to wear the whole uniforms-skirt thing and, you know, you had to go to mass every month or so. . . . And you would have religion classes, and you would have to write about the mass you went to, the homily, and also the gospel. . . . I remember that I would just take a missalette and I would just sit and daydream. That was my big thing; I was a big daydreamer. . . . I started to do drama in 7th grade and I really liked it. I went to a coed Catholic high school and continued to do drama, and that was my thing. I was like a theater nut. That was my niche, which was a relief, actually.

Although Candy found theater to be a good outlet for her talent and interests, she also learned about the power that teachers can have on supporting or dashing students' dreams.

I always got beat out by this one girl, Sherry, who always got the lead role. . . . It started me thinking about how our drama coach was also an English teacher, and it started me thinking, "Why was he treating me certain ways?" I was starting to really reflect on how my teachers were treating me and how I was looking more at our relationship, and I just was not feeling good about the relationship that I had with him. . . . I felt like I couldn't achieve goals and I couldn't really explore where I wanted to go. . . . We never really did drama *in* the classroom. We never did anything that I could feel like I could really excel at. . . . So that really started me thinking about . . . that wasn't such a positive experience and how that has affected me and does it affect others the same way. . . . It just started that whole questioning.

Candy's questioning about her own education became a catalyst for her desire to teach.

[I started to consider teaching] partly because of the negative experiences that I had, and also I was noticing when I started to really work with children after college that they seemed to have a natural affinity for drama and just role playing. . . . I was just, I was excited by that and I thought I'd like to transfer my negative experiences into making more positive experiences for . . . kids.

Candy took a somewhat circuitous route to TFD. After graduating from college, she went to California to be an actress. She lived in California for three months before deciding that acting just wasn't for her. She next went to Kansas to live with her mother and worked part-time at a local arts center. There she taught creative drama to children and became even more intrigued with teaching. Her full-time work was in banking. Later she returned to her home state and worked for a professional theater company. Next, she moved to a major midwestern city and worked in a bank for three years. She also returned to graduate school to earn a master's degree in theater and drama. She found that the only thing she liked about the program was the one course dealing with children and drama. While waiting to apply to TFD, Candy worked with emotionally disturbed children at a local middle school.

Kyla

Kyla grew up in a small midwestern city. She represented the second generation of her family to go to college. Although her father became a university professor, her grandfather was a farmer with an 8th grade education. She remembered her early schooling as a positive experience, filled with caring teachers. However, by middle school Kyla saw her teachers differently.

> Junior high [I had] terrible teachers [who] just had no vision, and I can't remember anybody who inspired me or anything like that. High school was just a little better.

Kyla was the middle of three daughters in her family and seemed to relish the idea of the "anonymity" that position gave her.

[Being in the] middle is a good thing for me. Usually it's not good, but I kind of like not having the focus on me quite as much. You know, some people crave it and I just didn't much. So I just kind of had this interest in social issues or a little bit of politics, but it was very unfocused or unclear and stuff so I went to [a major state university] first and ran for student senate. [Later] I transferred to [another major state university] and was part of the Young Democrats, where I was a part of anti-apartheid demonstrations [and other causes].

Kyla majored in political science and interned for her local congressman in the state capital and later for another congressman in Washington, D.C. Although she was interested in a variety of political issues, her work was mostly secretarial. From Washington she moved to New York and entered social work school. She soon became frustrated with the paradox of working in one of the most complex, diverse cities in the world while attending a program that seemed to ignore or fear that complexity and diversity.

[The program had] some kind of concentration you could take . . . they called CO (community organizing) . . . but it was an insult. It just was odd, you know it was like you're a giver and they're the receiver. . . . [We had] a really nice office at my placement, and they'd send us out in [a] car service to some project somewhere and you'd get out and go in. It was just absurd. It was absurd. . . . I understood that was for our safety. . . . I don't even know what it should have been instead, but it was just wrong.

Kyla challenged the idea that young do-gooders could meet the pressing needs of people who were a part of the city's welfare system. She also questioned the way social workers were prepared. More important, she questioned her own efficacy in this work.

> I worked with this family in the welfare hotel on 28th Street and Lexington, which was like, if you think about it, I mean it's not wrong. It's just that I was like a semi-midwesterner, you know, who looked rich because I was going to [graduate school], even though I was getting aid and going to this family. She [the mother] was HIV positive, and she had four kids, and they were just in this terribly dark, awful apartment, or hotel room. . . . When I finished my placement there, they got into some crappy apartment somewhere or whatever but they wanted me to counsel them, and I was just like totally unprepared to do that.

Later Kyla left social work school and joined an informal seminar where she read the works of Sol Alinsky and Paulo Freire. She got the opportunity to meet other community organizers and grassroots political workers. The seminar allowed Kyla to participate in a variety of community-organizing activities. In order to support herself Kyla worked as a waitress, but she loved working in the community.

> It was like the perfect kind of coalition of people, working with people, people developing a political and social agenda. I had to kind of work my way in there. I waitressed . . . and worked part-time . . . and eventually I got hired full-time.

Marcy

Marcy lived her entire life in the university town. Her father is a teacher; several other relatives, including her grandmother, had been teachers. She recognized that her life was relatively sheltered and that she lacked exposure to people who were different from her.

> I grew up mainly with white friends. The first time I ever came in contact with an African American teacher was 1st grade, and that was just a big deal because, like I said, we just didn't experience that. The one thing I remember in high school, that's when I really realized how, I mean it took 'til high school to realize how segregated people still were in the lunchrooms. . . . But it just really hit me because I always thought I knew different people and I had African American friends, but I just thought I was nonprejudiced. I thought I was very well grounded and aware of things, but I was fooling myself.

Marcy attended the university because it was cheaper for her as a state resident. Her initial interests were in public relations, but she especially enjoyed working with children. During her summers she worked as a softball umpire for the city's recreational program; as a senior in high school she was a part of a drug awareness program where she spoke with 6th graders. After college, Marcy was a conference coordinator and meeting planner for a national student services organization. To help her make her decision about entering teaching, Marcy, like Robin and Candy, took a job as an educational assistant where she questioned the logic of a school system that prescribed a one-size-fits-all curriculum for its students.

> I mainly worked with [students on] reading and writing. . . . But the strategies [the classroom teacher] showed me, I don't think would necessarily work with every kid. They had the attitude that all of their [strategies] work with all kids. That's [their] atti-

tude and that's not the case. I mean, going back to the curriculum, that you have to get something and just totally tear it apart and say, "OK, this will work or I can stretch this out here."

During the TFD program Marcy began to recognize her own transformation. She acknowledged that her own social privilege limited her perspective and that she needed to broaden her view of the world.

I think that I'm more knowledgeable, or not necessarily knowledgeable but just aware of all of these differences . . . between schools and kids and abilities. I think beforehand I was very open-minded about it, but I think I just had a more narrow vision of what it was really like based on my experiences.

Diana

Diana is a Latina who grew up in the northeastern United States. She admits that she lived a life of relative privilege and was uncomfortable being cast in the role of "disadvantaged minority," which clearly some people tried to saddle her with. Diana went to an Ivy League university—the same university her father had attended. Her father was a college professor, and her mother was a science teacher in a private school. She seemed to find her identity through music and performing.

Starting really early on I got involved in a children's theater organization . . . a collaborative group. We all had different roles in there. . . . It kind of helped me . . . working in children's theater helped me kind of come to, I mean it was sort of like an identity-forming thing. It was the first time I had really taken a leadership role, and it kind of showed me that I

had some . . . proclivity [for] something besides music. . . .
I was very musical as I was growing up.

After college, where she majored in anthropology, Diana
moved around and worked a variety of jobs. She moved to
Hawaii hoping to work in children's theater but ended up being
a waitress. Later she moved to California where she worked at a
YMCA after-school program. Within a relatively short time she
was asked to serve as program director, and for almost two and
one-half years she ran the after-school programs. Next, she
added the responsibility of directing the morning kindergarten
program. When her partner decided to return to graduate
school, they looked at schools on the East Coast and in the Midwest. When they came to the Midwest, Diana took a job at the
YMCA and directed two programs that served kindergarten-
aged children.

Diana chose TFD because she enjoyed teaching (based on
her YMCA experiences) and because of its emphasis on teaching children who were traditionally underserved in school.

I grew up in [name of town], a very middle-class town, and I
think very quickly I began to resent that because as soon as
I was allowed to . . . I started going into bigger places. . . .
It wasn't just like everyone was the same . . . and it felt a lot
more accepting to someone who was having this adolescent
struggle of who am I, and so bigger cities have definitely had
an attraction for me. In [name of town] the population that I
worked with was primarily African American. The bilingual
classroom that I worked in was Spanish-English bilingual.

Diana also chose the program because of some of her own
identity concerns.

I've always had issues around my father being Cuban, my mom being European American . . . we spoke English around the house. We lived far away from my Cuban relatives . . . and I've always wanted to surround myself with people that have a more [positive identification] with [Latino] cultures.

This snapshot of the 1996 cohort (see Table 2.1 for a synopsis) is a brief introduction to the women who were willing to be studied while they completed their elementary teaching certification and master's degrees. Snapshots like this one, however, cannot begin to capture the complexity of their lives and depth of their various life influences on them. It is as if the reader sees a group of people in a photo and asks, "Who are they?" The

Table 2.1. Teach for Diversity Cohort.

Name	Race-Ethnicity	Family Background	Undergraduate Major	Prior Work Experiences
Vanessa	African American	Working class	Psychology	Instructional aide
Tara	European American	Middle class	Japanese	Instructional aide
Robin	European American	Middle class	Political Science	Alaskan fishing boat; instructional aide
Brenda	European American	Middle class	Rehabilitation Psychology	Occupational therapist
Candy	European American	Middle class	Drama	Acting, banking, instructional aide
Kyla	European American	Middle class	Political Science	Community organizer
Marcy	European American	Middle class	Communication	Instructional aide
Diana	Cuban American	Middle class	Anthropology	Community center teacher

response is likely to be, "That's Jim; he's my Uncle Ed's son; that's Liz, my best friend." Now the viewer has identity labels but no access to the true identities. Such identities unfold over time. Throughout the book, I elaborate further on the novice teachers' lives and pedagogy, the point being to help teachers and teacher educators recognize the "relatives" of exemplary beginners.

The common element the cohort shares is that each member is female. Two of the eight are women of color; seven come from middle-class backgrounds, although Kyla pointed out that her family is only two generations away from its farming background. None of the women majored in education, although Brenda attempted to enter the elementary education program and was not accepted. Her default major became rehabilitation psychology. All of the women took advantage of the opportunity to work with people in a teaching-learning environment. All except Brenda had previously worked with school-aged children.

TFD Under Way

Each TFD student was told that research is an important component of the program. However, the ethical tenets of research meant that no TFD participant was required to participate in research, and no one was to participate without signing an informed consent form. My colleagues and I knew that we wanted to do some research on the TFD program. Each of us has our own research agenda. The first year the program was so new and we were spending so much time putting out fires that we had no time to develop a program of research. We were too busy running a program.

During the second summer for the first cohort, we admitted the students in the second cohort. We decided to ask members of the first cohort to meet with the new cohort to share their perspectives about the program and offer advice. Four members of the first cohort agreed to attend the new cohort's seminar. One piece of advice was that the new cohort should learn to lean and depend on each other because the intensity of the program would require them to cooperate. The members of the Hughes cohort heard that message loud and clear.

In the Fall each school site cohort formed its own seminar, which was led by a faculty member. In the Hughes cohort we decided to read Martin Haberman's book, *Star Teachers of Children in Poverty*.[2] Each student agreed to read a chapter to share with the group. Near the end of the book, the students decided to do something that signaled to me that they were indeed a group, not just eight individuals trying to get teaching certificates. At one of our seminar meetings near the end of the semester, the Hughes cohort shared a video they had created. Vanessa got her mother to let them use her school one Saturday, and they produced a hilarious spoof of the book. Watching the video I could see how much these young women liked each other. They were having a good time, not just completing an assignment. As the video played they laughed and teased each other. They were in this thing together, and it seemed to me that they might make an ideal group to study.

I had experienced a number of concerns with my first-year cohort. I counseled one member out of the program; another experienced a serious illness and took a leave of absence. Two other members had personal issues that made them poor candidates for participating in a long-term study project.

But the year-two cohort was convivial and collegial. They worked well together, and it seemed they also played well together. Not long after they were placed at Hughes, they began meeting for drinks on Fridays after school. Their closeness was apparent in the other classes as well. The entire twenty-five-member TFD cohort took their methods courses together. The Douglas cohort, however, was dealing with the stress of a political decision that was about to affect the entire school community. The Lafayette cohort was struggling with some problems tied to its school organization. There were not enough single classrooms, and some of the students had to be assigned to "specials" teachers (for example, computer lab, art, or music) for part of their assignment. The Hughes cohort members, however, had a relatively smooth transition to their school site, and they enjoyed the placement. Each time the entire group gathered, the Hughes members chose to sit together and continue their camaraderie.

In the chapters that follow I tell a collective story of the novice teachers' struggles to do the best possible job of teaching all of the students. I make no attempt to address each teacher equally. Instead, my goal is to tell a richly textured story of what it means to become a teacher in a program devoted to preparing teachers for diverse classrooms.

The next chapter describes one of the three tenets of culturally relevant pedagogy—academic achievement—and how the novice teachers worked to ensure that all of the students were learning.

3

They're Supposed to Learn Something

> Too many of our best and brightest have been
> rendered virtually inaccessible to us largely
> because they have experienced too much
> schooling and too little education.
> —*Mwalimu Shujaa*[1]

During my first year of teaching I often went home asking myself, "Did my kids learn anything today?" I was so busy trying to manage the clerical and bureaucratic tasks and keep my students in some sort of "order" that I'm not sure how much teaching and learning was taking place. Sure, there were many days when my principal or district supervisor came into the room and the students were busily working on something. But what was its educational value? Did that task push students intellectually? Or did it just make me look like I was in charge?

Schools' New Responsibilities

Our nation's schools are charged with increasing responsibilities for our children, including their health and welfare in addition to their education. Because public schools are so central to students' (and their families') lives, state, federal, and local governments use them to address any number of society's public concerns. For instance, many children get some portion of their health immunizations at school. Millions of students receive meals (breakfast and lunch) at school. This social welfare function of schooling is not unique or recent.[2] In our contemporary society schools have extended their scope of responsibility. Not only do schools help students with physical needs such as health and food but they are now called on to deal explicitly with students' emotional and psychological needs.[3]

In fairness, some of the health and welfare concerns that schools address are well founded. Indeed, former principal Madeline Cartwright[4] insists that the school must deal with *anything* that gets in the way of children's learning. If students are hungry, ill clothed, sick, or suffering from emotional or psychological trauma, and these issues impede students' learning, the school must take steps to eradicate these problems. My argument is not that pressing human needs must be ignored by schools and teachers but that teachers cannot forget their primary mission—helping students learn.

> More than a third of the students in my first classes were African American children bused to the school's working-class white, ethnic neighborhood. The students had to get up by 5:30 A.M. to catch a bus that left before 7:00 A.M. Most of the students arrived each morning hungry and tired. Before long I found myself buying cereal, milk, and juice and offering a "voluntary breakfast." Most of the bused kids began eating breakfast. They were putting in twelve-hour days (from the time they got up until the time they returned home), and the only meal they had was the USDA lunch.

Schools' Primary Task

No matter what else the schools find themselves doing, promoting students' academic achievement is among their primary functions. At its best this notion of academic achievement represents intellectual growth and the ability to participate in the production of knowledge.

If intellectual growth is to be ensured, someone must be able to attest to a student's academic progress. Did a youngster come into a class unable to read? Did she leave that same class still not able to read? How can we argue that academic achievement has occurred? And high-quality academic achievement means that students are capable of doing something with knowledge other than repeating and reproducing it.

A clear example of the distinction between consuming knowledge and producing it is seen in the very different ways that students in high-income schools use computers, compared to the way their counterparts in poor schools use them.[5] In upper-middle-class schools students use computers to produce mathematical and scientific models. They learn to develop graphs, presentations, videos, and various forms of media. In poor communities, if students have access to computers—and many do not—they are often asked to use the computer like an electronic workbook. The computer asks the questions and the student responds. Tasks are rarely intellectually demanding, and the machine controls the interaction.

Despite the variation in the quality of intellectual work offered in different schools, the point still remains: students are supposed to learn something in school. Students of color have a distinguished history of striving for academic excellence, despite very long odds.[6] However, the current performance of some students of color suggests that education is not a priority for them. Indeed, Fordham and Ogbu[7] argue that high-achieving African American high school students were chided by their peers for attempting to "act white"—a notion that caused quite a stir in the educational community. Some might argue that schools began to use this as a convenient excuse for being unable to raise the academic achievement levels of African American students.

But I argue that students develop their academic identities long before they arrive at high school. From the time students start school, they begin to learn their academic and social roles. These roles are determined by which reading groups students are assigned to, which special or compensatory education services they receive, and what opportunities they have to display knowledge in the classroom. By the time students enter high school, these academic and social roles have become fixed and immutable. Indeed, when working-class or poor students of color see a student who looks like them participating in something like an honors program, the orchestra, or the chess club, they are justifiably curious about how that happened. "What are you doing over there with them?" is a logical and legitimate question, based on the deeply ingrained and structurally reinforced notion that only white students and some students of Asian descent do "those" things.

One of the first things I attempted to teach my 8th graders was Shakespeare's play, "Romeo and Juliet." "Those kids can't read Shakespeare," my colleagues insisted. I was undaunted. I had heard too many complaints from the kids about how boring the reading was. I introduced the play by asking, "How many of you have a brother or sister who has a boyfriend or girlfriend that your parents hate?" Almost half the hands went up. "Well, what does your brother or sister do?" I began to hear all kinds of stories about kids sneaking out to meet dates, sneaking phone calls, and meeting at football games or movies. From there we began to talk about popular music that discussed "forbidden love." Next, we watched "West Side Story" and then a film version of "Romeo and Juliet." Before long the kids were begging to read the book. They wanted to read this story for themselves. It probably took us twice as long as a high school class to read it, but we read it all the same.

Why Students Don't Achieve

A variety of alternate hypotheses can be offered to explain why some students of color continue to reject school-based academic achievement. One hypothesis is that students of color merely reflect the rejection of academic achievement and intellectual pursuits so evident in the larger U.S. culture. Americans tend to be suspicious of people who are highly intelligent, preferring instead what we term *well-rounded* students—those whose grades are a bit above average, who play a sport and possibly an instrument. The academic superstars are seen as anomalies and are not to be emulated.

A second hypothesis argues that some students of color fail to achieve because they cannot see the value of investing time and energy in academic pursuits. Even though we constantly prod students to do well in school so they can "get a good job," many students have figured out that success in schools does not necessarily equal a good job. In many low-income and working-class communities, students can point to numerous examples of people who went to school and persisted, yet they have no job (or have a job that is not commensurate with their level of education). From statistics that determine the value of a high school diploma, we learn that, on average, whites with high school diplomas earn significantly more than African Americans with the same credentials.[8]

A third hypothesis is that working-class and poor students know others like them who did not achieve in school or did not persist yet are materially successful. In a consumer-driven culture where fast cars, fancy clothes, and expensive jewelry are the markers of success, young people are easily seduced by material gain, even if the ability to consume comes as a result of sports (to the detriment of a real education) or illegal activities. The challenge for teachers is to help students *choose* academic achievement in the face of powerful and competing alternatives.

Definitions of Achievement

Focusing on academic achievement means certain things for teachers and students. More specifically, in a classroom where the teacher focuses on academic achievement

- The teacher has clear goals for student learning and achievement.
- The majority of the class time is devoted to teaching and learning.
- The teacher (not only a standardized test) assesses student learning.
- The teacher can articulate individual student progress.
- The teacher is knowledgeable and skillful.

The Hughes Cohort and Academic Achievement

In the next sections I describe the school setting and some instances where novice teachers from the Hughes TFD cohort demonstrate their commitment to the academic achievement of all students.

The Hughes Setting

The members of the TFD cohort arrived at Langston Hughes Elementary School about a week before school began. They began their year at Hughes by attending the faculty-staff potluck at the principal's home. In a short time, the Hughes cohort began mingling with their new colleagues and mentors; early the next morning they began preparing to become teachers.

Langston Hughes School is located in a working-class community and serves about four hundred students in grades pre-K through 5. Most of the students are eligible for free or reduced-cost lunch. The school has a growing English-as-a-Second-Language (ESL) program for its Latino and Hmong students. Although the Hughes community contains mostly modest, single-family homes, it also includes a housing project where many of the low-income students and students of color (African American, Latino, and Hmong) live.

A core of teachers at Hughes are committed to child-centered pedagogy. Their classrooms reflect a more "open" approach to teaching where children make lots of decisions about their learning; others teach in a more traditional way. Their teaching is more directive. However, this book is not about evaluating teaching styles. It is about understanding how novice teachers learn to be good teachers in classrooms serving diverse groups of students.

Cohort Members' Assignments

Vanessa worked in a 3rd grade classroom with a cooperating teacher who had been at the school for several years. Her class of about twenty-three students had white, African American, and Latino students; one East Indian student spoke very little English. The classroom was fairly traditional, focusing on improving students' basic skills—reading, writing, and mathematics.

Tara worked in a 4th and 5th grade classroom with a cooperating teacher who was very interested in science. Each year she entered her students in a citywide science exploration. The cooperating teacher's style was student-centered; she encouraged the students to create a democratic classroom. The class included African American and white students and was exceptional because only nine girls were in it. From the first day, Tara was faced with an energetic group of students who were ready to challenge her at every turn.

Robin worked in a 2nd and 3rd grade classroom. Her teacher gave her carte blanche in determining how she would work with the students. The cooperating teacher's style was rather open and student-centered. There were white, African American, and Hmong students in her class. Many of her students received special services such as ESL instruction and Chapter I or Title I reading and mathematics support.

Brenda began the year in a 1st grade classroom with about twenty-two students. The skills she had acquired while working with developmentally disabled adults stood her in good stead as she worked with children who were struggling to learn the alphabet and some of the rudiments of reading. After the first semester Brenda switched to working in two classrooms; she was in a kindergarten and 1st grade classroom in the mornings and co-taught with Robin in the afternoons.

Candy also changed classrooms at midyear. She began teaching in a 4th and 5th grade classroom in which eight students identified as "emotionally disturbed" were placed. Along with the cooperating teacher, a special education teacher spent most of her time in the classroom. After some prodding, Candy was convinced to work in a 1st and 2nd grade classroom where she was able to use many of her drama techniques. Both teachers Candy worked with had a more student-centered approach to teaching.

Marcy worked in a 4th and 5th grade classroom with a cooperating teacher who taught in a more traditional, teacher-centered way. However, the teacher worked to cultivate a strong sense of independence in his students. Although she was nervous about starting out with "older kids," Marcy quickly became comfortable; her class included white, African American, Latino, and Hmong students.

Diana worked in a 2nd and 3rd grade classroom with a Latina cooperating teacher. The class was a mix of student- and teacher-centered instruction. Diana quickly became comfortable in the setting of white, African American, and Latino students.

Kyla worked in a 2nd and 3rd grade classroom with a cooperating teacher who had an outstanding reputation for her progressive approach to teaching. The class was made up of white, African American, Latino, and biracial students. Students in this class were expected to (and did) take responsibility for curriculum development and classroom management.

> My own student teaching placements couldn't have been more different. The first placement was at a suburban school. The entire school population, the teachers, and administrator were white. The curriculum and teaching was scripted. The cooperating teacher handed me a list of what to teach, when to teach it, and urged me to watch her to see how to teach it. My "creative" ideas were nicely dismissed and everyone was bored to tears.
>
> My second placement was in what would now be called the inner city. The students were lively and energetic. The teacher, Mrs. Reid, was indeed, a master teacher who urged me to use my imagination. "You've got to keep the kids' minds working so their bodies don't start!" It was her way of telling me that early adolescents needed to be intellectually engaged or I was going to have classroom management and discipline problems.

Tying the Curriculum to Real Life

The Hughes TFD cohort had interesting ideas about how to support the academic achievement of the students in their classrooms. Candy argued that "using drama in the classroom provides a natural way for a child to learn all the curriculum."[9] Diana said that it was her "aim to treat all . . . children with equal respect, and to help them respect . . . [their] own heritage as well as that of others. With this as the basis for my teaching I have been seeking new ways to incorporate a more rigorous curriculum into the [elementary program]." However, it was Kyla's statement that fit comfortably within the TFD philosophy. "In Latin, 'to teach' means 'to draw out.' The operating assumption . . . is that people have it in them, and that it is a matter of creating the environment for people to develop their gifts and talent. . . . My assumption is that talent is there in children."

Kyla's belief in a more Freirian[10] approach to teaching and learning was congruent with her cooperating teacher's philosophy. Their school year began with a new student, Latrice, an African American girl who had transferred from another school in the district. Although Latrice was only a 3rd grader, her mom was very worried about recent changes in Latrice's attitude and behavior. She was beginning to hang around some older girls who lived in their apartment complex. Latrice swaggered into Kyla's classroom declaring that she was "in charge."

A Recycling Unit

Kyla soon learned that Latrice was unable to read and also struggled in math. In her first solo effort in the classroom, Kyla decided to initiate a unit on recycling. The topic was timely, and it was something in which all of the children could participate. As a part of the unit, the students would build a compost heap (science), read books and write stories about conservation, ecology, and the environment (literacy), calculate the amount of waste that was being produced in their classroom (mathematics), and invite speakers from the State Department of Natural

Resources and other conservation agencies into the classroom (social studies). One of the major projects of the unit was to collect aluminum cans to raise money for a project or charity that the children decided on.

Many of the students loved the unit, especially being able to play in the compost heaps. They asked interesting and provocative questions. However, some of the children seemed less enthusiastic about the recycling unit. One student who was obviously disengaged was Latrice. "Why we gotta collect trash? I don't wanna be no garbage collector!" Latrice resisted any attempt to get her engaged in the unit. Another student, Winston, also seemed to be uninterested. In one of the class discussions, Winston informed the class that his father collected cans to earn money. Quickly Kyla realized that her "class project" had the potential to eat into the family income of one of the children in the class.

Instead of scrapping the unit or ignoring the issue, Kyla telephoned the father to discuss what the class was doing. The father agreed to talk with the class and did so. His visit was a big hit. He explained to the students how he went about can collecting, where the best places were for finding cans, and how to carry large numbers of cans. However, the students were shocked when they learned how low the exchange rate was for aluminum cans.

An AIDS Unit

On her next unit, Kyla worked closely with her cooperating teacher to teach a unit of AIDS. The cooperating teacher had successfully taught this unit before and encouraged Kyla to participate fully. Despite the children's young age, the unit dealt openly and honestly with this difficult subject area at an appropriate instructional level. The unit involved the school nurse, students' parents and other relatives, and the children themselves. Ultimately, the cooperating teacher and a colleague (from another school) produced a videotape of the unit; children and adults talked about why they thought it was important for kids to learn about AIDS.[11] Two of the people prominently featured in the video are Latrice and her mother. The viewer learns that Latrice's grandmother died of AIDS, and this class was the first in-school (and perhaps out-of-school) environment where she felt safe enough to discuss it.

The AIDS unit became something of an academic watershed for Latrice. She wanted to read everything she could about the topic. She willingly wrote stories about AIDS. One clip of her in the video shows her diligently counting the money the class raised to contribute to an AIDS support network charity. Perhaps the biggest lesson that Kyla learned from this experience was that students' academic achievement is intimately tied to the things they care about. They learn what they love.

A Literacy Unit

Diana seemed to be tooling along in her classroom. Her cooperating teacher was well organized and a good planner. Diana's transition into the class was smooth. Her initial responsibilities were to conduct the daily writing workshop. She fell into the program easily and was enjoying herself.

Soon her cooperating teacher challenged her to come up with some activities of her own. At first Diana was at a loss as to what to do. She was concerned about how to plan activities that met the wide range of abilities of the students in the class. She was particularly concerned about Warren, an African American 3rd grader who was struggling in literacy. Like many students who are challenged academically, Warren spent much of his time in class avoiding work. His name was regularly on the teachers' lips. "Warren, sit down. Warren, finish your work. Warren, pay attention." Diana knew that she wanted Warren to be able to benefit more from instruction and developed a project that she believed would be an excellent hook. She had witnessed Warren's rapt engagement whenever he attempted to make something. He had no problems concentrating in art or when he was working on a project of his own.

Diana decided to read the book *Gallimoto*[12] to the class. The story describes an African boy in Malawi who wants to build a gallimoto. Throughout the story the students try to determine what a gallimoto is. They finally learn that it is a kind of model cart made from wire. After reading the story, Diana told the students that they too would be making gallimotos. Warren was delighted by the chance to build a gallimoto, and this activity served as an important catalyst for his academic engagement. Diana realized that it would do no good to constantly hound Warren about working. It was her responsibility to find ways to get Warren to choose academic activities. A quality that was apparent in the Hughes cohort teachers was their ability to think through difficult academic issues and ensure that the students in their classes focused on their academic responsibilities.

Handling "Problem" Children

Vanessa's classroom was organized very differently from Kyla's. In Kyla's classroom students participated in planning the curriculum; in Vanessa's the planning was done by the cooperating teacher, with some input from Vanessa. Vanessa planned her own lessons, but she was required to do them within the context of the cooperating teacher's long-range plans.

Marcus

One of Vanessa's challenges was dealing with Marcus, an African American boy who had been identified as having learning disabilities. Marcus's academic success became part of Vanessa's special mission.

> I [was] kind of looking out for African American kids, especially the African American males in the school. I would see them in the office a lot. It was interesting because I kind of made it a point for them to know me and know who I was. They'd go through the hall, "Hi Miss Willis, hi Miss Willis," because I think that [it is possible for] people who don't have the privilege of going through a program [like TFD] and have some of those stereotypes, especially about African American males and "their behavior problems," and because they get labeled so.

But Vanessa's concern with Marcus was not a misplaced romantic notion about racial or cultural solidarity. She made academic demands on him that he had not faced before.

> I think that I really clicked with Marcus, but . . . it was a real struggle. It was a real love-hate kind of relationship. He liked me one day. [He hated me the next]. "I love you Miss Willis; I hate you Miss Willis." I think that came [because] I was trying to be more strict with him. I thought he was given [too much] flexibility and a lot of leeway on things. He had some special circumstances, you know his father died [this year] . . . but I felt it was time for him to kind of get back into the groove of things and continue on [academically]. After a while he started to use that flexibility to his advantage. You know, when there was something that he [didn't] want to do in the classroom he said he had a headache. [The cooperating teacher] let him go to the nurse to lie down. But he would

always get back up when it was time for recess, and there were no consequences [to him]. [But I would say], "OK, if you have a headache now, I'm not punishing you but you need to get this work done, so we'll spend a certain amount of time during your recess [finishing your work].

Tiffany

Another concern that Vanessa had was with Tiffany, an African American girl who was very bright but struggling within the structure of this classroom. For the two previous years Tiffany had been in a more open-structured classroom where she flourished. Her parents were excited about her academic progress. However, this classroom seemed too rigid for Tiffany. She seemed to always be on the wrong side of the class rules. She was used to moving freely around the classroom, asking provocative questions, reading interesting and challenging books. The cooperating teacher felt that Tiffany was immature and perhaps had a learning disability. Vanessa believed that Tiffany was one of the strongest students in the class.

At the first parent-teacher conference the cooperating teacher voiced her concerns to Tiffany's parents. The look on their faces as they left the room showed their devastation. Vanessa rushed out to catch them in the corridor and told them that her conclusion was just the opposite. The cooperating teacher saw this exchange and may have read it as disloyalty or a conspiracy of sorts. Unlike many of the students in our regular teacher education program, Vanessa was not willing to "go along to get along." She was willing to take a stand when it counted.

I don't want my class to be a place where clones are made . . . where I want everyone to do this at those certain times, and it's so structured that there's no flexibility for the students or for students that have different ways of learning. There is no alternative for them. You know, you read the book now for twenty minutes, then you do the report. I don't want that at all. . . . I don't want a classroom where students are afraid of me because I'm the authority in the classroom. They're scared to ask me a question because they think it's stupid or because they think I'm going to get upset or it's not the appropriate time.

Jerome

Brenda stood more than six feet tall, and her statuesque countenance seemed out of place in a 1st grade classroom. However, she moved with ease in and around the six- and seven-year-old children. It was not unusual to find her sitting on the floor among them. One of her students, Jerome, was a twin (his brother, Tyrone, was in another class at Hughes) who was struggling to learn to read. Although most of the other children knew all of the letters of the alphabet, Jerome was still unable to identify letters and sounds. Jerome hated reading time because it made his shortcomings public. Most days he acted out just enough to be excluded from the group. "Jerome, go sit at your table," was a phrase uttered regularly by the cooperating teacher.

Once Brenda figured out that Jerome was cleverly disguising his limitations, she came up with a plan to bring him up to speed without embarrassing him. She created a small set of cards through which she punched holes and connected them with a binder ring. Each card had a letter of the alphabet on it—uppercase on one side, lowercase on the other. Brenda showed Jerome how he could slip the binder ring on his finger and flip through the cards whenever he needed to know a letter. This ready reference became an important tool for Jerome. Before long, he depended on the cards less and less. Brenda understood that he needed a chance to succeed and that it was her job as a teacher to find a way for him to do so.

Brenda's earlier experiences with people facing all kinds of challenges made it easy for her to consider alternate ways to support students' success. She worked as a tutor for children who were learning English. She worked with low-income women from diverse cultures who were displaced homemakers. She worked with people (and their families) who had Alzheimer's disease. She worked with people who had sustained industrial injuries. She also worked with a man with cerebral palsy, teaching him how to do his job of encoding checks in a bank.

For Brenda the issue was not whether a student can be successful but what supports teachers must provide to ensure that success.

> I've learned that I've got a lot more to learn with teaching, that's for sure. I've learned that when you're in the classroom . . . you have to include everyone in what you're trying to do. You include the people that you're working with in what you're trying to do. Otherwise, you're just kind of going through the motions.

Brenda also worried about the substance of learning that took place in the classroom, and she was developing a metacognitive perspective to her teaching:

> You do all these fun things, but OK now, what did they learn? What am I trying to get across? What are my goals for that? I think I had to look back and say, "OK, here are my goals and how do I get them" . . . whereas, before [the things I did were] really basically work-oriented. [I have to say] "these are our work goals and we're going to try and get you here on time."

> In one of those strange quirks of big city school districts I found myself teaching a 2nd grade class one year. It was a strange

experience because I had grown accustomed to working with middle school students. However, after transferring to a school closer to my home, I ended up in a primary classroom. I thought the kids were aliens. Why did they cry over every little thing? Why did it take them all afternoon to copy their homework from the board? Why can't they take their own coats and boots off? But an amazing discovery I made while teaching these little folks was that they were incredibly bright. Whenever I placed an intellectual challenge in front of them, they gobbled it up. They weren't afraid to be wrong. They loved to use their minds. One day I decided to really make them stretch and started teaching them Spanish. Within a few days the children were greeting me and their classmates in Spanish, "Hola, maestra. Como esta usted?" Five years later (after I had left the school to return to graduate school) I ran into one of the parents. "Do you know that Jonathan hasn't been challenged like that since he was in 2nd grade? Why don't teachers think the kids can learn?"

That parent's question, asked of me almost thirty years ago, remains salient today. "Why don't teachers think the kids can learn?" I am often asked to conduct professional development in schools throughout the nation. When I share some of the wonderful things I have seen exemplary teachers do in their classrooms, I regularly hear comments like, "Well, my students can't do that." "We don't have the necessary parent support to do that kind of work." We can't give our kids homework; they won't do it." I am dismayed and angered by the powerlessness expressed by many teachers. Why do a job that can't be done?

The Sins of the Parents

The novice teachers in this study focused on what they could do, not what they couldn't. In our postobservation conferences and seminars the cohort members regularly looked at how problems might be solved. They did not worry about whether the students' parents could participate actively in their education. Instead, they asked themselves, "What else could I be doing to support this student's learning?"

However, a few years ago I had an opportunity to invite some university colleagues from various fields (law, medicine, arts, and sciences) to visit a local high school. Part of our tour included visits to a variety of classrooms. My colleagues noticed a disturbing pattern in the classes. The more challenging courses—AP biology, precalculus, Latin—were filled with white, middle-class students, as well as students of Asian descent. The less-rigorous courses—basic English, life science, general math—had plenty of African American and Latino students. In the AP biology course white, middle-class students spent time in a well-equipped lab conducting sophisticated experiments. Across the hall in the basic science class, a group of African American and Latino students were doing "experiments" with household cleaners! At a debriefing session one of my colleagues, who is a scientist, asked why the kids in basic science were working with cleanser, pine oil, and ammonia. The teacher remarked, indignantly, "Well, those kids' parents don't participate in the school."

Most of my colleagues sat dumbfounded. They could not believe what they were hearing—that students' academic opportunities were being circumscribed by their parents' ability to participate in the school. But I knew that the teacher's sentiments were not too different from those of many others. Increasingly, children are being asked to pay for the "sins" of their parents. If students are poor, with parents who do not have much education, they are at a decided disadvantage in the classroom.

A disturbing trend in early childhood education is the expectation that young children (in kindergarten and 1st grade) will come to school already knowing how to read. This trend means that children who cannot read are often treated as though they do not deserve to be instructed. In his early research, Rist[13] documented repeated instances where the most educationally needy students actually received less instruction. It was no coincidence that those same students were the most economically disadvantaged.

Indicators of Academic Achievement

Although the narratives of the novice teachers of the Hughes TFD cohort help explain what it means to focus on academic achievement, it may be more helpful for teachers to examine statements of what academic achievement is and then apply those statements to their own practice. In my view, then, academic achievement is evident in classrooms where

- The teacher presumes that all students are capable of being educated.
- The teacher clearly delineates what achievement means in the context of his or her classroom.
- The teacher knows the content, the learner, and how to teach content to the learner.
- The teacher supports a critical consciousness toward the curriculum.
- The teacher encourages academic achievement as a complex conception not amenable to a single, static measurement.

• *The teacher presumes all students are capable of being educated.* This indicator is an important starting point for culturally relevant teachers. Instead of presuming that intellectual ability is limited to those students who have already benefited from the society by virtue of their race, class, or gender, presuming all students can be educated orients teachers toward supporting the educational success of all students. When students are struggling to be academically successful, the teacher asks questions about what adjustments she needs to make to ensure that success.

  • *The teacher clearly delineates what achievement means in the context of his or her classroom.* Sometimes students do not receive a clear message about what it means to be successful in the classroom. In a study of literacy for early learners[14] teachers were surprised to hear their kindergarten and 1st grade students explain that good readers were people who sat up straight, listened to the teacher, and didn't talk. Somehow the teachers had conveyed to the students that being a good reader was related to classroom deportment. In the classroom of a culturally relevant teacher, the students know exactly what success entails. They receive a variety of information from the teacher about what matters academically.

  • *The teacher knows the content, the learner, and how to teach content to the learner.* Shulman[15] outlines the components of good pedagogy as content knowledge, pedagogical knowledge, and pedagogical content knowledge. In my conception of culturally relevant pedagogy these components are reflected in the academic achievement proposition of the theory. Certainly, every teacher should know the content. Elementary teachers need to know enough mathematics, English, science, and social studies to provide rigorous intellectual experiences for their students. They also need to know their students and know how their students learn. Finally, they need to know the unique aspects of teaching particular subjects. How one teaches mathematics is different from how one teaches history. Culturally relevant teachers adjust their teaching to meet the demands of both the learners and the subject matter disciplines.

• *The teacher supports a critical consciousness toward the curriculum.* In this era of standards-based school reform, few teachers are asked to take a critical stance toward the curriculum. Most are expected to accept the curriculum (or standards) as a given and teach whatever is necessary to ensure that students perform successfully on district- or state-mandated tests. However, culturally relevant teachers know that for students to exhibit any power over their own lives they will need to be critical about information, including the information contained in textbooks, electronic media, and other forms of content. Helping students raise critical questions and search for multiple perspectives is an important aspect of academic achievement.

• *The teacher encourages academic achievement as a complex conception not amenable to a single, static measurement.* We are living in an era of unprecedented, high-stakes testing for children in schools. Many school districts make determinations about whether children can be promoted to the next grade based on a single, norm-referenced, test score. This get-tough policy flies in the face of everything we know about testing and assessment. In the classroom of a culturally relevant teacher, academic achievement is measured through a variety of means. Students have an opportunity to demonstrate what they know and are able to do through samples of their work, performances, and exhibitions. These teachers also allow students multiple opportunities for academic success. No one-time assessment seals the academic fate of students.

In the next chapter I discuss the second proposition of culturally relevant teaching, cultural competence, and how the new teachers incorporated it into their practice.

4

Nobody Wants to Be Urkel

We real cool. We
Left school. We

Lurk late. We
Strike straight. We

Sing sin. We
Thin gin. We

Jazz June. We
Die soon.

—Gwendolyn Brooks[1]

Javier was a very bright student. He was an excellent reader and asked good questions. He had a real talent for analysis. But he never did his homework and usually came to class unprepared—no books, no paper, nothing to write with. Working with him was frustrating. I knew he could be the intellectual leader of the class, but he did not seem to want that.

I began watching Javier in noninstructional settings. He was popular. He was a good dancer and smooth with the girls. The most important thing in his life was being cool. When I realized that, I understood that I had to approach Javier in a different way. I asked him to meet with me after class one day:

"What's going on with you, Javier?"

"What do you mean Miz L.?"

"I know you're smart but you're acting like you don't want to succeed?"

"Aww. I can't be actin' like no 'school boy.' If my boys think I'm a punk, I won't hold no more check in this school."

"So what if I gave you a way to be successful without looking like a schoolboy?"

"What do ya mean?"

"What if I give you another set of books to keep at home and you won't have to carry books here. The other set will already be here."

After Javier agreed to the arrangement, he began to soar academically. He was reading and doing his assignments at home, but his friends didn't know that. This arrangement allowed Javier to be an academic achiever who maintained his own sense of himself as a young African American man.

In other writing[2] I have said that cultural competence refers to the ability of students to grow in understanding and respect of their own cultures. What we typically see in schools where students of color are academically successful is a growing alienation of the students from their home cultures. This alienation may occur because so little of the schooling experience embraces the cultures of students of color. Indeed, much of what some cultures (for example, African American, Latino, American Indian) value culturally is rendered illegitimate in schools.

Most teachers have little or no genuine experience with cultures different from their own. Although many teacher education programs offer courses, workshops, and modules that address multicultural education, these offerings tend to be superficial and tangential to the real lives of students. Although most of these programs are aimed at "exposing students" to other cultures, they rarely involve a close look at the assumptions, worldviews, and perspectives that prospective teachers come with.

As Gordon[3] has argued:

Teachers and the teacher education field are in need of a fundamental critique of how they look at, interpret, and assist people of color in the educational process. Such a critique will require fundamental shifts in the frameworks through which teachers view themselves and others in the world, not only in the paradigms they employ and validate in their teachings, but also in a willingness to acknowledge the credibility of other perspectives, particularly those that challenge comfortable, long held assumptions [p. 20].

When I worked with prospective teachers in an undergraduate teacher education program, I asked the students if they could identify an adolescent, male, African American, series television character who exemplified academic excellence. The most common response was the character "Steve Urkel" of the then-popular television program, "Family Matters." Most of the students agreed that Urkel was a cultural incompetent. Although he was an extremely smart teenager, it was clear that no other African American adolescents wanted to associate with him. Ultimately, the situation comedy writers created a kind of alter ego for the Urkel character (Stephon Urkelle) who was considered "cool"; much less emphasis was placed on his intellect and academic abilities.

Students of color often struggle with what they see as diverse and competing perspectives—to be smart or to be cool.[4] These perspectives are not only made dichotomous by students but they seem to exist as opposite ends of a continuum in the larger society. Our heroes in sports, entertainment, and even politics tend not to showcase their intellect but instead to opt for a more "common folks" persona—one that says, "See, I'm just like you."

For students of color, the "you" that students strive to be "just like" may not clearly demonstrate an intellectual side. Michael Jordan has become a shrewd business man, but his celebrity and attraction for young people emanated from his ability to fly through the air and slam dunk a basketball while wearing a pair of really cool sneakers. Students abhor the "nerd" image of Urkel and gravitate to the cool, hip, and even dangerous images of superstar athletes and entertainers.

But the rejection of the nerd and the nerd image is only half the story. Those students of color who are academic achievers may find themselves in the position of rejecting the cultural representations displayed by their lower-achieving peers. For example, in an urban school desegregation program African American students were bused to the suburbs. Once they arrived in the suburbs the students who succeeded academically began a slow but steady process of detaching themselves from many of their cultural markers. The students began changing the music they listened to, their hairstyles, their clothing, and their speech patterns. Instead of the more familiar African American vernacular, their informal language was peppered with the suburban "up-talk"[5] of their white peers.

It is true that all teenagers want to fit in and, like all human beings, adapt to new environments. But the pattern of change was most evident among the high achievers. Not only were they attempting to fit it but they were making an assessment about what it took to be *perceived as successful*. Tatum[6] points out that in most racially mixed high schools in the United States, one can walk into the cafeteria and find a table filled with only black students. The white students are all sitting together too, but this decision of African American (or Latino or South East Asian) students to sit together may represent an attempt to maintain a sense of cultural competence.

Although I had an opportunity to attend an Ivy League university, I chose to attend a historically black college. My white classmates could not understand such a decision. "I never heard of that college you're going to," remarked Aaron Rubenstein. "I can't believe you're turning down a chance to go to Penn," said Barb Lazarus. "You're making a big mistake." I wish I could say that my white classmates' comments didn't matter, but they did. I was nervous about my choice but there was a voice inside that kept telling me that I was making the right decision. I had proven I could compete in a highly academic setting. I ended up ranked number 14 out of a class of 450. But I was more terrified of losing my sense of who I was. I was also tired of fighting white students—not physical altercations but the daily verbal sparring where they demonstrated their not-so-subtle contempt for my presence in honors classrooms. When I got to college and looked around the campus, in the dining hall, throughout the dormitory, in the classrooms, and saw almost nothing but black faces, I experienced the first real relief in school I had had since 6th grade.

The Importance of Culture

The average white teacher has no idea what it feels like to be a numerical or political minority in the classroom. The pervasiveness of whiteness makes the experience of most teachers an accepted norm. White teachers don't understand what it means to "be ashy" or to be willing to fail a physical education class because of what swimming will do to your hair. Most white teachers have never heard of the "Black National Anthem," let alone know the words to the song. Most have never tasted sweet potato pie or watched the intricate process of hair braiding that many African American girls (and increasingly boys) go through. And although African American youth culture has become increasingly popular, and everyone can be heard to say, "You go, girl," and believes she has the right to sing the blues, the amount of genuine contact these people have with African Americans and their culture is limited.

Similarly, the growing Latino population has forced a change in popular culture. Ricky Martin, Christina Aguilera, Enrique Iglesias all are enjoying huge popular success. But most white teachers cannot speak even rudimentary Spanish—enough even to signal an emergency or satisfy a basic need. More disturbing is the way Latinos are racialized into a unitary category. Few teachers (and prospective teachers) know the distinctive histories of Mexican Americans, Puerto Ricans, Cuban Americans, El Salvadorans, Guatemalans, Peruvians or the countless others who originate in the Spanish-speaking Americas.

The indictment is not against the teachers. It is against the kind of education they receive. The prospective teachers with whom I have worked generally express a sincere desire to work with "all kinds of kids." They tell me that they want to make sure that the white children they teach learn to be fair and to get along with people different from themselves. But where is the evidence that the prospective teachers can get along with people different from themselves? When asked, most of my students admit that they have never gone to a movie or shared a meal or visited the home of a peer who is racially or culturally different. Some, because of program requirements or their own faith commitments, have worked in a soup kitchen or shelter or in other "helping" roles with people different from themselves. But these brief forays into the lives of "others" often serve to cement the impression that others are always needy and disadvantaged.

"Helping the less fortunate" can become a lens through which teachers see their role. Gone is the need to really help students become educated enough to develop intellectual, political, cultural, and economic independence. Such an approach to teaching diverse groups of students renders their culture irrelevant. There is nothing there to be learned, let alone built upon and developed. Certainly, every group has some "worthies" like Martin Luther King Jr. or Cesar Chavez, but even these cultural heroes have become sanitized to meet normative standards.[7] Students are encouraged to be like (Martin Luther King Jr., Cesar Chavez, Sojourner Truth, Dolores Huerta, and so on) because they were "good Americans." Rarely are students invited to learn about the way such people stood up to America (not just to a "few bad people") and demanded that the country live up to its own democratic rhetoric.

Culture is a complex concept, and few teachers have an opportunity to learn about it. Most teacher education programs are founded on the social science discipline of psychology (and some sociology). Rarely do prospective teachers examine education through the discipline of anthropology. And although it is important for teachers to understand their students' culture, the real benefit in understanding culture is to understand its impact on our own lives. Thus, the TFD program was interested in helping prospective teachers look at the way their cultural background influences and shapes the way they understand and act in the world.

Some teachers assume that the "right" way for students and their parents to respond to school is the way they (and their parents) responded to school. When parents fail to come to school and participate in school activities, teachers may assume that the parents don't care about education. Teachers (like all of us) may attribute meanings to parents' and students' behaviors that are incorrect. For example, if an upper-middle-income parent sends her child to school late because she is rushing to her high-powered job, teachers may express more sympathy and understanding for the parent's situation. However, a working-class or poor parent whose child comes to school late may be perceived as someone who doesn't value education. How is it that the very same behaviors evoke radically different responses from teachers? This is an issue of the teacher's culture and social expectations, not the student's (or the parent's).

The Cohort's Understanding of Culture

The TFD student teachers from the Hughes cohort demonstrated an acceptance of students' cultures and their desires to be culturally competent. Their statements of purpose reflect this acceptance.

Tara

Tara's high school experiences in Japan gave her a powerful example of being outside the dominant culture. In her statement of purpose, she said:

> When I was in Japan I was startled into a new worldview. I no longer saw things quite the same as before. For instance, the language itself guided me toward new kinds of thinking, since Japanese is predicated on a complex hierarchical structure. This allowed me to react and interact with people in different ways than I had before.

In addition to her changed worldview, Tara also experienced discrimination in Japan. In culturally homogeneous Japan, Tara's blonde hair and freckles made her very different. She experienced being ridiculed and being ostracized. Soon she began changing in ways that made her seem less American and more Japanese. In some of her photographs of her time in Japan we saw Tara dressed in traditional dress (kimono) and school uniforms. Her hairstyle and facial expression mimic that of the Japanese students. Tara worked on reinventing herself to fit in. Her own culture became a burden in Japan.

As a teacher she gravitated to the students who seemed to be on the fringes of the classroom community. Her relationship with Terrance was filled with tension. However, she empathized with Terrance because she knew what it felt like to hate school and to be different from the other kids. Similarly, her relationship with Jamie, a student who was struggling with math, demonstrated her sense of empathy and care for the students.

> I discovered that humor was a really good tool and [Jamie] understands metaphor really well, which is a wonderful thing when you're trying to get a child to get beyond the situation. [Jamie] was by far the most math-phobic child I had ever seen. . . . I thought I was math-phobic, but at least I would do it. Jamie would just get so worked up . . . and then he would just lose it. . . . [But I tried] to make sure [school] was in the context of fun. Jamie is one of those artsy people, and he's got a really great imagination and school doesn't tap in on that enough for him.

Robin

Robin became more aware of her culture when she began to travel. She had lived in various parts of the United States (Detroit, Seattle, Alaska) and the world (Spain, England, Puerto Rico). She had also traveled briefly to Mexico, Portugal, Morocco, France, Italy, Holland, Austria, Germany, and

Jamaica. She said, "The most vivid memory I have was living in a foreign country and not being able to express myself as I'd like. It was a trying and humbling experience."

Robin also reflected on the experiences she had while living for seven months aboard a fishing boat in Alaska:

> This . . . taught me not only about different cultures and customs, as my fellow crew mates hailed from all over the world, but also about accepting diverse attitudes and values. Many of my crewmates were ex-convicts, recovering alcoholics, con artists, [and] chauvinists. . . . Learning to accept people on their own terms and refraining from judgment took a while, but in the end enabled me to know people truly different from myself. Empathy took on new meaning—I haven't personally felt the hardships that some others have, but I now have friends that have dealt with similar hardships and I can relate better. . . . [A]fter becoming close to someone that was in prison five years and having him share his experiences, like when he told his mother he was going to prison and "breaking her heart," I felt I had gained a more open mind—one not limited by labels.

Kyla

Kyla was right up-front with who she was and what that might mean. Her statement of purpose included the following:

> I am a twenty-nine-year-old white woman, newly married and recently transplanted to [this town] after seven years on the East Coast. Although I was undoubtedly shaped by being brought up in . . . a conservative, homogeneous town, I was fortunate enough to have parents who felt it important that

I have experiences with people of other races, religions, and economic groups—people who were different from us. Mom led a Girl Scout troop on the south side of town, made up of lower-income, African American girls. Mom and Dad took me on "HELP" calls where we drove elderly, disabled, or poor people to appointments or for groceries.

Kyla's early experiences with people of various backgrounds helped to shape her later career choices—first in social work and then in teaching. From the moment that Kyla walked into her assigned classroom, she was comfortable with the students. After twenty years of supervising student teachers I recognize certain aspects of their demeanor. Kyla's face did not reveal the fear or the pity I often witness in the faces of novice teachers. She was not afraid to touch the children and be touched by them. She was warm and open and friendly, but she was not trying to be their "friend." She understood that she was there to be a teacher, and sometimes that meant that she had to make decisions that children did not like.

One morning while observing in her class I saw that Kyla was having a struggle with "Justis," a small, African American boy who was struggling to learn to read and write. Justis was a self-proclaimed "tough guy" and very skilled at avoiding work. But with Kyla, Justis could not get away with that. She understood that he had to maintain his dignity, but the bottom line was that he had to do his work. She did not shout at him or try to intimidate him, but she was persistent in her requests. "Justis, you need to do this," Kyla said. "I can't," Justis insisted. "Yes you can," said Kyla. Then a tear tumbled from Justis's eye. Kyla leaned close to him and whispered, "Justis, there is no reason for you to cry. Either get started on your work now or you will have to do it at recess, but you will do it."

Kyla understood the twin goals of helping Justis achieve while allowing him to maintain his sense of himself. Within a few minutes Justis began to wipe his eyes and attempt to complete his work. Kyla quickly went over, sat by his side, and gave him the one-on-one instruction he needed.

Vanessa

Vanessa understood better than the rest of the cohort members that the students of color were walking a fine line between their school identities and their home identities. Most of the students wanted to do well in school. They wanted the approval of their teachers. But schools are places that *give* students an academic identity. The teacher who regularly praises the work of certain students is telling them and their peers that they are smart. Conversely, the teacher who never praises students or who denigrates students' efforts is telling the students that they are not smart and not intellectually capable.

Vanessa had seen the influence of school on students' lives in her own schooling experience. In her statement of purpose she said:

> I have witnessed the lives of classmates and others around me falling apart without the intervention of the community or helping professionals. This caused me to begin to question what I could do to assist children who are lacking the support and direction needed.

The African American children in her class were delighted to have her there. At one point she considered changing classrooms, but her dedication to the children kept her there despite some philosophical differences between her and the cooperating teacher.

Sometimes I wanted to leave because I don't think I want to work in a classroom that is quite that structured. I want to be more innovative and creative in the classroom. But I needed to stay there. . . . There was one incident when a [white] student . . . called me out of my name. Some students said that he [used] the N word. Other students said that he didn't, so you know, I don't know what was said because I wasn't there to hear it. . . . He did have other problems with an African American girl in the classroom when he said that whites were better than blacks, and so we had already had kind of a racial thing going with him. We [he and I] had to sit down and talk about why he felt that way; when it really got down to the bottom of it, he had heard his dad say that and he just brought it back into school as fact.

Vanessa's decision to stick it out in the classroom demonstrated her commitment to all of the children in her class. She wanted all of the students, regardless of their racial or ethnic background, to see that she, an African American woman, could be an excellent teacher. She wanted to help the students of color see that there was a wider array of social roles they could play beyond the dichotomous ones of geek versus cool. She also understood that her presence in the school could be helpful for all of the students:

I would find myself in the classroom and in other people's classrooms and just in this school in general, kind of looking out for the African American kids, especially the African American males in the school. I would see them in the office a lot. It was interesting because I kind of made it a point for them to know me and know who I was. They'd go through the hall, "Hi Miss Willis, hi Miss Willis."

Vanessa may also have felt an added burden of having to demonstrate to her cohort peers that she was as capable as they were.

> Even some of the people from the cohort were like, "I don't want you to think that I'm coming to you because you are African American," but that [was] the primary reason. [They would say] "what should I do if so and so says this, or what does this mean? One of the cohort [members] called me and was like, "Don't get mad, but I need some rap music and I was wondering if you had some rap music." I was like now . . . why am I the only one who has rap music?

As the TFD program progressed, Vanessa found a way to make her concerns known about being the only African American in the cohort. The other cohort members began to see that Vanessa was not responsible for educating them about African American culture. Little by little the cohort saw that although Vanessa may have had some cultural advantages with African American students, she had many questions about the Latino and Asian-descent students in her classroom.

Marcy

Marcy grew up in the university community and described herself as "being in her own little world" there. She was bright, popular, and attractive. She knew little about the world of children whose lives were not like her life, but she learned about what it means to be on the margins through her interactions with one of her students, "Lucas."

> [Lucas] was in his third school. He's a 4th grader and had just moved here. . . . He was very behind in reading and writing,

and I just tried to work with him and talk with him. . . . I had him come in sometimes, and he wanted to eventually come on his own . . . maybe for fifteen minutes at lunch or at a recess and read with me or do something. He was very vocal and . . . he had a great imagination and loved to talk. . . . Kids teased him because he said things that didn't always seem like the most popular thing to say or the right thing to say in the eyes of [the rest of the] kids.

Marcy's ability to work and empathize with Lucas represented something of a breakthrough for her. Although she clearly had compassion for students in Lucas's situation, she did not really know how effective she might be with them. However, she was determined to support him academically while trying to make sure that other students regarded him as a full member of their classroom community.

By her own admission, working with children who did not live in stable households was new to Marcy. If students moved constantly from school to school, how were they going to make friends and establish trust with adults? Marcy realized that the answer to working with Lucas was not by trying to be like him or holding her own experience up as the way things should be. Rather, Marcy learned that success with Lucas would come through allowing him to be himself. She listened to him. She asked him questions about himself. She made herself available to him, and she found ways to insert herself into his life. More important, Marcy never considered giving up on Lucas as an option.

Cohort Members' "Difficult" Students

Another cohort member, Candy, also learned some powerful lessons about students living in difficult situations.

Bobby

One of her students, Bobby, was diagnosed as having severe emotional disabilities. It was not uncommon for Bobby to become frustrated with school work, throw his work down, and scream at the teacher. He (along with several other students in the classroom) required the services of a special educator in the classroom along with the regular education teacher. Sometimes the special educator found herself in a confrontation with Bobby because she insisted that he do (or not do) something. These confrontations often ended badly. Candy tried a different approach. She tried to talk with Bobby when he had classroom outbursts. She knelt down to be face to face with him and spoke softly:

> Candy: Bobby, what happened?
> Bobby: I don' know.
> Candy: Why are you so angry?
> Bobby: I can't do this!
> Candy: OK, so you're angry about this work.
> Bobby: I'm stupid!
> Candy: If you were stupid, do you think you'd be here in 5th grade?
> Bobby: I don' know.
> Candy: Well, I do know. This is a classroom where people are supposed to learn. It's not a place where everything is supposed to come easy. How can I help you with this work?

Reluctantly, Bobby agreed to try again with Candy's help. But all of her interactions with Bobby were not successful. Sometimes he remained as angry and obstinate with Candy as he was with the special educator. The difference I noticed between Candy and the special educator was that Candy seemed to rack her brain to figure out what else she might do to be successful with Bobby.

During one of our postobservation conferences when Candy had had a particularly difficult time with Bobby, she was on the verge of tears. My initial interpretation was that she was embarrassed that I was witnessing her struggle. But as we talked she said, "I don't expect to be perfect. Heck, at this early stage of the game I don't even expect to be good. I'm concerned that I'm not thinking this situation with Bobby through well enough. I don't want this to be an ongoing situation. I want to get better at working with him."

Myron

Candy was experiencing success with another "difficult" student in the class, Myron. Myron was an African American boy who had struggled to be academically and socially successful in the classroom. In previous years, Myron was regularly sent to the office and the time-out room because of his behavior. The vicious cycle of poor school performance as a catalyst to poor school behavior was emblematic of Myron's school experiences. Myron was one of the other students in the class who received the services of the special educator.

Each day the special educator literally held Myron's hand as he walked through the corridors to and from special classes (art, music, physical education), from the classroom to the cafeteria, and from the playground to the classroom. Myron was visibly uncomfortable with this arrangement; often the hand holding was accompanied by his struggling to get free. Candy studied Myron carefully and decided that she would approach working with him differently.

The advantage that Candy had over the special educator in working with Myron was that Candy had met Myron during her summer placement at the local community center. Each day during the summer she saw Myron as a happy, inventive, and sometimes mischievous boy. He was popular and a leader. The Myron of the community center looked nothing like the Myron of the classroom. Candy's quest was to unravel the mystery of the "two Myrons." What was happening in school to make a relatively capable boy seem incompetent?

> I know he's no angel, but I certainly don't think he's emotionally disturbed. I've seen him work well with other people, be cooperative, be a leader. . . . I realize I'm just learning how to be a teacher, but my hunch is that calling him emotionally disturbed is just a convenient way of not really dealing with him. I'm not convinced that Myron is failing. I think *we're* failing.

Because Candy knew that Myron was imaginative and that the typical school curriculum failed to capitalize on his imagination, she decided to work with Myron on some drama activities. Although her attempts to get Myron to act were a struggle, she persisted. By the time she left the classroom to work in a primary classroom, Myron had committed to appearing in a school play. At the performance of the play I attended, I was as intrigued by Candy's reaction as I was by Myron's performance. He played the role of a policeman, and he was magnificent. His voice was loud and clear, and he seemed a natural in the role. In the play Myron was no longer the kid whose hands had to be held by the teacher. He was no longer the problem boy. Now he was Myron the actor, and the entire school got a chance to see him being successful in this new role.

Candy's eyes stayed glued to Myron. A slight smile graced her lips as he recited his lines. Before the performance was over I saw tears glistening in Candy's eyes. Although she was student teaching in a new classroom, she continued to feel a strong sense of responsibility toward the students in her first classroom. At the end of the performance Candy rushed over to me and said excitedly, "Did you see him? Did you see Myron? Wasn't he great?" Her joy was unmistakable. It was honest and sincere and pure. It was the kind of reaction that happens when an adult really cares about a child.

In my first teaching job I came home exhausted every night. Part of the exhaustion was tied to how difficult the job was, and part was tied to my lack of competence. It took me twice as long to do things that experienced teachers did. Simple tasks like taking attendance were a mystery to me. I couldn't figure out the excuse codes. I didn't have a system for efficiently collecting homework. I couldn't keep the tardy policy straight. More important than my problems with juggling the clerical tasks of teaching was my problem with Dennis.

Dennis was an African American boy who could light up the room with his smile and could just as easily destroy the room with his anger. He had been in a series of foster homes and even more schools. With all this moving around Dennis never learned to read. In fact, he struggled to do almost every school task, so he rarely attempted any of them. Instead, he spent his time trying to disrupt other students from doing their work.

My task became trying to figure out what might serve as a hook for Dennis. It didn't have to be an academic task. It just had to be something that he found engaging. The academics could come later.

As our social studies class began studying life and customs during colonial times, someone asked a question about how the colonists entertained themselves. When I suggested that dancing was one form of entertainment, Dennis perked up. "What kind of dancing?" At that moment, I knew we would incorporate dancing into the unit. We learned reels and minuets and early forms of square dancing. Dancing became Dennis's reason for coming to school. It was my firsthand experience with providing an education that capitalized on those things that students care deeply about. Dancing allowed Dennis to be himself and continue to learn. I wrote out the directions to the dances, and Dennis worked hard to learn to read the directions. It was the first interest he had shown in an academic task.

Helping students become culturally competent is not an easy task. First, it requires that teachers themselves be aware of their own culture and its role in their lives. Typically, white middle-class prospective teachers have little or no understanding of their own culture. Notions of whiteness are taken for granted. They rarely are interrogated.[8] But being white is not merely about biology. It is about choosing a system of privilege and power. The white ethnic students in my first teaching job called themselves Italian or Irish or Polish. Their working-class backgrounds made it difficult, if not impossible, for them to identify with whiteness. In our current society people with ethnic and cultural identities often find themselves *choosing* whiteness over those identities. Such a choice comes at a cost.

I gave a lecture at a local community college when a young man approached me at the end of the question-and-answer period and said, "You said a lot about Native American history and African American history and Asian American history, but what about white history—what about *my* history?"

I followed up with a question that seemed to startle the young man. "Are you white?" I asked. "Or do you have an ethnic or cultural heritage other than white?" He responded by saying, "I'm Irish." I then began to tell him about some of the aspects of Irish history—how the Irish were the first group the British exploited for slave labor in the Americas.[9] I told him about the intricate clan structure the Irish had developed that allowed them to hold land in common and prevent exploitation. The young man knew nothing of this. I was not surprised. I suggested that he did not know his history because, somewhere along the line, his family may have chosen whiteness over all else. And when one chooses whiteness as a primary identity, one's ethnic and cultural history disappears. All he has left to signal his existence is something about a potato famine and St. Patrick's Day.

It would be simplistic and wrong to suggest that cultural and ethnic identities are fixed and discrete. Few Americans have a pure heritage or identity. But the customs and traditions we observe, the people with whom we associate, and the ideas we cultivate all shape our identities; in a society that places such priority on *racial* identity, we are naïve if we attempt to ignore race. Indeed, ignoring race may prove to be a dangerous decision for some.

Teachers who are prepared to help students become culturally competent are themselves culturally competent. They do not spend their time trying to be hip and cool and "down" with their students. They know enough about students' cultural and individual life circumstances to be able to communicate well with them. They understand the need to *study the students* because they believe there is something there worth learning. They know that students who have the academic and cultural wherewithal to succeed in school without losing their identities are better prepared to be of service to others; in a democracy this commitment to the public good is paramount.

Indicators of Cultural Competence

It is important to provide some specific indicators of cultural competence for teachers—both preservice and inservice—to determine how they might improve their practice.

Cultural competence occurs in classrooms where

- The teacher understands culture and its role in education.
- The teacher takes responsibility for learning about students' culture and community.
- The teacher uses student culture as a basis for learning.
- The teacher promotes a flexible use of students' local and global culture.

- *The teacher understands culture and its role in education.* Earlier in this chapter I discussed the idea that many teachers do not understand the role of culture in education. Often teachers attribute pseudopsychological explanations to students' school struggles. For example, many teachers are quick to say a student does not do well because she has low self-esteem or lacks motivation when they actually know nothing about determining levels of self-esteem or motivation. Similarly, teachers use *culture* as a generic term to mean *different from them.* Culturally relevant teachers understand that culture is a complex concept that affects every aspect of life. Such teachers are able to recognize their own cultural perspectives and biases.

- *The teacher takes responsibility for learning about students' culture and community.* Students do not come with instruction manuals. Each classroom and each student presents a new set of opportunities and challenges. And there is as much diversity within a group of students in a classroom as there is between them and another group of children from a different racial, cultural, socioeconomic, or language group. However, people living together in a community share certain social rules and conventions. People with shared histories may respond similarly to life's challenges. Language binds people together in special ways.

How are teachers supposed to learn the codes and norms of a community different from their own? Too often teachers rely on the distortions of the larger society to explain a new cultural setting to them. Or teachers rely on the interpretations of more veteran teachers who may have never ventured out into the school community. The teachers' lounge becomes a place of misinformation. In some schools where the faculty is made up of teachers of color and white teachers, the two groups of teachers rarely interact. One group may use the lounge; the other may congregate elsewhere. Much like Tatum's[10] reflections on teenagers who are working toward racial identity development, teachers are also confronted with their racial and cultural identity when they work in communities of color.

Culturally relevant teachers know that it is their job to learn about the students' cultures and their communities. They need to bridge the divide between the school and the students' homes. They do not assume that students have to learn their ways and rules. They understand that the interest they show in students' backgrounds and lives has an important payoff in the classroom.

• *The teacher uses student culture as a basis for learning.* In a middle-income, white, English-speaking school community, teachers *do* use student culture as a basis for learning. It is relatively simple to use middle-class white culture as a basis for learning because the curriculum, interaction styles, speech codes, and school norms are congruent with students' home culture. But when students' home and community cultures deviate from the school norms, what do teachers do?

Culturally relevant teachers understand that learning is facilitated when we capitalize on learners' prior knowledge. Rather than seeing students' culture as an impediment to learning, it becomes the vehicle through which they can acquire the official knowledge and skills of the school curriculum. However, in order to capitalize on students' cultures, teachers have to know the students' cultures.

• *The teacher promotes a flexible use of students' local and global culture*. Human beings are complex. Our cultural affiliations are nested and multifaceted, and the cultural categories we use are crude approximations of individuals' cultures. When a teacher uses a cultural event or activity to represent every member of that culture, she may be assuming cultural affiliations that students do not share. For example, a cultural event such as the African American holiday Kwanzaa may be as strange to African American children as it is to non–African American children. Asian American children may feel no affiliation with people and customs from specific Asian nations.

Culturally relevant teachers know enough about the students they are teaching to help students make use of their multiple cultural identities. Those identities may span racial, ethnic, and national boundaries.

———

In the next chapter I discuss the ways the Hughes cohort members developed the third aspect of culturally relevant teaching—sociopolitical consciousness—during their fifteen months in the TFD program. I share some of their insights about this aspect of their preparation and ways it affected their thinking about teaching.

5

Apathy Is Not an Option

> The obligation of anyone who thinks of himself as responsible is to examine society and try to change it and to fight it—at no matter what risk. This is the only hope society has. This is the only way societies change.
>
> —*James Baldwin*[1]

Like many new teachers I thought the only thing I had to take responsibility for was ensuring that the students were successful with the curriculum and felt reasonably "good" about themselves. I had a number of political commitments. I was active in the civil rights movement. I attended rallies, read radical texts, and supported the whole gamut of social justice causes. I just kept those things separate from my life as a teacher. I was incensed about the war in Vietnam and even more exercised over the slow progress of the fight for African American liberation. But I thought it was "not my place" to bring my politics into the classroom.

By 1972 the Watergate scandal was in the news, and the Nixon White House was unraveling in full view of the nation and my students. "I knew Nixon was a crook all along," remarked Victor, an Afro-Latino boy in my history class. "I don't know why they're even having a trial. That boy is guilty!" Victor's comments echoed those of many people in communities of color. Sammy Davis Jr. notwithstanding, Nixon was never a favorite among people of color. But

Victor's comments made me realize how important it was to help students get a better grasp of where their political opinions and ideologies come from. I checked out a television set from the media center and began showing students the congressional hearings. To my surprise their comments and perspectives on the proceedings were insightful and perceptive. They asked good questions and made powerful inferences. They liked debating the issues and appreciated knowing how different aspects of the government functioned to facilitate the process. No textbook could ever have provided this kind of education.

Schools as Teachers of Social Justice

The concept of school as a site of social justice education has a long tradition in communities of color. In African American communities this work is well documented. The college students who were on the front lines of civil disobedience in the form of sit-ins and other types of social protests were prepared for that social action on their various campuses.[2] School became a place to learn about the responsibilities of citizenship in a society that was structured by racial inequity. The work of increasing voter registration among African Americans in the South was supported by the creation of Citizenship Schools, initially staffed by members of the Highlander Folk School.[3] This work started with helping African American adults become literate so that they could register to vote. It continued with various "graduates" of the Citizenship Schools, such as Fannie Lou Hamer, becoming the next generation of teachers in schools throughout the South.[4]

The students who formed the Student Non-Violent Coordinating Committee (SNCC) also developed schools during the time they were organizing African American communities to register to vote and participate in civil disobedience against the apartheid conditions of the South. SNCC called its schools Freedom Schools and assisted young people with basic skills in literacy because they were unable to obtain adequate education in the segregated and underfunded schools in their communities.[5]

By the time a segment of SNCC evolved into the Black Panther Party, the notion of school as a site of social action was institutionalized in the civil rights (or black liberation) movement. Although much of the public perception of the Black Panthers is about militancy and violence, the organization included programs designed to feed and educate children. Of course, the education that students received in the Black Panther–sponsored schools was a radical political one, intended to support the liberation of black people.[6]

More current examples of schools and teachers with social action components also exist in the literature. Tate[7] describes a math teacher in a city where zoning regulations meant that some areas of the city were wet (they allowed liquor sales) and other areas were dry. Not surprisingly, schools serving low-income, African American, and Latino students were located in wet areas. After her students complained about constantly being hassled by the patrons of liquor stores and bars, the teacher got the students involved in a project that consisted of examining the zoning laws. The students took field trips and learned that schools in more resource-rich communities tended to be in dry areas. The students made observations in their own school community and documented the number of liquor stores in a short radius of their school. Ultimately, the students worked on proposals for rezoning to present to the city council.

Torres-Guzman[8] describes the social action work of high school students in an alternative school setting. The students began investigating what they termed *environmental racism* in

their community. They documented the dumping of toxic sub-
stances in their Latino community and dubbed themselves the
Toxic Avengers. The project both promoted student engagement and improved academic skills.

Sociopolitical Learning in TFD

As faculty we planned TFD to be more than a teacher certification program. Although elementary teacher certification was
one outcome of the program, we were also asking teachers to
function as change agents in a society that is deeply divided
along racial, ethnic, cultural, linguistic, and class lines. To fulfill
this function, we needed to develop a program that would support teachers' sociopolitical learning.

Service learning is one of the latest innovations in schooling.[9] Many high schools require students to participate in some
aspect of service as a condition of graduation. As is true with any
school-supervised activity, the quality of service learning programs exists on a continuum from terrible to excellent. Clearly,
some programs give students an opportunity to serve and learn.
However, students experience other programs as merely another
set of obstacles to negotiate. If graduation is contingent on accu-
mulating service hours, then students in some programs focus on
completing the hours. They may place less focus on the quality
of the experience, and not much learning or service occurs.

In TFD we knew that we wanted students engaged with the
community in some meaningful way. We wanted them to both
learn and serve because our conception of teaching was that it is
a service learning profession. Our conversations about the specific kind of community service ran the gamut from constructing
a tightly structured experience to allowing students carte
blanche.

My own experience with community service in teacher education came during an earlier teacher education program. My initial full-time teacher education position was at a small Catholic university that ostensibly had a social justice mission. However, many of the social justice projects promoted by the institution took place in international settings. The university administrators seemed to relish the idea of "doing something" in El Salvador or Guatemala but were oblivious to the social justice concerns across the street. The campus was filled with Latino gardeners and custodians but had few Latino students. The campus dining halls had African American cooks but almost no African American students or faculty. However, one of the faculty (a priest) decided to initiate a campuswide program of community service. This program was unattached to any specific school or department, but individual faculty could connect the program with their courses.

I decided to use the university community service program as a part of my courses. Students were required to spend six to ten hours per week in community service. Some of them had wonderful experiences where they learned about the realities of social inequities in the society. One student did her community service at a homeless shelter. In addition to helping distribute blankets to the clients, she created a role for herself by using her musical talents to play the piano in the common room. However, one of the regular residents seemed to resent her piano playing. Finally, the student and the resident had a confrontation. She learned that the resident's irritation was because he felt that her piano technique was poor. "Scoot over," the resident barked. The student complied and within a minute she was enraptured by a beautiful Bach concerto. "It was like this guy could've been at Julliard or something. I was thinking he's just some homeless loser, and he was a better pianist than anyone I'd ever heard. The whole thing made me think about how it was possible that someone with that much talent could end up in a homeless shelter."

The student's experience was a wonderful opening that allowed her to challenge notions of meritocracy extant in the society. However, not every student experienced a social justice epiphany during the community service component of the course. Another student did her community service in a free day-care program that was set up for displaced homemakers and immigrant women. Although she enjoyed working with the children, she seemed to have no empathy or compassion for their mothers. Her work in the day-care program reinforced her idea that the mothers were somehow deficient and lacking in moral scruples. The student complained about how the mothers were "cheating" their children from the kind of "maternal nurturing" they needed to be successful.

The student's assumptions about the relationship between a particular type of maternal care and later success reflects a simplistic reasoning that probably is grounded in her misunderstanding and misinterpretation of principles of human development. Her analysis completely ignores the larger social and economic factors that impinge on individuals' lives and their life chances. The community service did little more than reinforce her ideas about the unworthiness and deficiencies of the children's mothers.

Using community service as a way to develop a greater sense of empathy and deeper feelings of respect for all humanity is problematic. Students need the opportunity to not only participate in community service but to receive help in understanding their community service. Knowledgeable faculty can work to help students interpret their experiences and prompt deeper thinking through the use of critical questions.

In TFD we developed both structured and less-structured service opportunities for the prospective teachers. The structured experiences occurred in the first summer of the program. We told the students about a variety of possible sites for their summer field experiences and asked them to select their first, second, and third choices. They were allowed to choose from a day camp for homeless children run by the Salvation Army, the local YMCA, various neighborhood center summer programs, and a very informal program run out of a set of apartments in a low-income community. Students spent six weeks in their community placements and were supervised by a university graduate student who was an experienced teacher and community activist. Each week during the summer the students met with my colleague and me to discuss their experiences and raise questions about the communities and their role in these community-based settings. Some of the prospective teachers were fortunate enough to do their community service at an agency close to the school where they would later prepare to be teachers.

During the school year, we expected the students to continue with a community service project. However, rather than assign the TFD students to community service during the year, I permitted the Hughes cohort to design their own community service. Because of my previous experiences with community service, I held a strong belief that students were more likely to benefit from a community service project they wanted to do. The guidelines for community service were broad. Students could do a project that involved developing a closer relationship with individual students, or they could do something that was aimed more toward supporting group goals.

Vanessa, Robin, Marcy, and Brenda did projects that involved becoming mentors for individual children. Tara, Kyla, Candy, and Diana chose projects that were more group-based, that is, projects that extended beyond the school and classroom. Vanessa decided to develop a mentoring relationship with Maya, an African American girl who was struggling to achieve in the classroom. One day a week Vanessa walked home with Maya and spent several hours at her apartment. They talked about Maya's aspirations—her hopes and dreams—and they talked about ways Vanessa could better support her in the classroom. Over time, not only Maya but her sisters looked forward to Vanessa's weekly visit.

Robin served as a mentor for Kenny,[10] a southeast Asian boy who was struggling to learn English. Kenny was an enigma. He talked with English-speaking classmates all the time, but his reading and writing skills were extremely poor. He went to ESL class each day for thirty to forty minutes. Robin was puzzled because she saw Kenny as a proficient English speaker. She did notice that almost all of Kenny's conversations were about television. He knew what time every program came on, and he used television as a marker for everything that happened in his life. For example, if his friends said they were going to soccer practice at 6:00, Kenny would say, "Oh, 6:00—'Simpsons.'"

Robin told Kenny's parents that she was spending time with him to tutor him, but her real motivation was to learn more about the language acquisition process. Robin understood that good community service involves reciprocal relationships. Not only was Robin helping but she was being helped. Over time she learned that what appeared to be English fluency in Kenny's oral language was actually Kenny's demonstration of his incredible memory. Kenny sat before the television set mesmerized, and as the characters on the various sitcoms, cartoons, and dramas recited their dialogue, Kenny repeated the words. Kenny could repeat large portions of dialogue from his favorite programs and movies. He also recited the dialogue with the accents of the characters. Kenny loved doing Arnold Schwarzenegger characters. "I'll be baaack!!" was one of his favorite sayings.

Tara's community service was work with the local adult lit-eracy council. She served as a literacy tutor for two adults—an African American man and a Latina. Once again the experience served as both a help to the community members and a benefit to the prospective teacher. The African American man that Tara tutored had difficulty decoding words but had a firm grasp of the meaning of the various texts she presented him with. The Latina could decode most of the words. She understood the sound-symbol relationship and could sound out most of the con-sonant and vowel sounds. However, she rarely understood what she had just "read." This experience was instrumental in helping Tara formulate her position on the reading debates. "It's really not a question of phonics versus whole language. These two peo-ple showed me that we are dealing with a much more complex set of problems. Teachers can't just depend on one set of strate-gies to help students learn to read."

Diana selected what seemed to be the most unorthodox community service activity. She served as a volunteer for a "parental stress hotline." Several hours a week Diana answered the frantic calls of parents who were struggling to parent. The benefit of serving as a hotline volunteer was that Diana became more sensitive to the demands placed on parents. When stu-dents were unable to complete homework assignments or follow through on other school-based responsibilities, Diana was not so quick to make judgments about the parents and their interest in their children's education and welfare.

Kyla had an interesting dilemma in deciding how to proceed with her project. Originally, she thought she might help Latrice, the African American girl who was struggling to read. But her thinking changed as she considered the way Latrice might be instructed in the classroom.

> I really wanted to help Latrice, but I started looking at what was happening to her in our class. She already had the Title I support person coming in to help her. Whenever we had parent volunteers, they helped Latrice. What message were we sending her? I was afraid that either she wouldn't even try because someone was always there to do it for her or that she would think that everybody thought she was too dumb to do anything. I decided helping Latrice was only going to make me feel better . . . it probably wasn't going to do much for her.

Rather than work solely with Latrice, Kyla decided to spend additional time at Hughes School three to four times a week. She set up a homework help club (although the children did not have conventional homework assignments) where students could go for additional help on papers and projects they were working on in class. For example, Kyla's cooperating teacher had her students work on a quarterly newsletter. The newsletter explained many of the projects and activities that were happening in the class and solicited parents' help for various new endeavors. Kyla made herself available to all of the students, and sometimes Latrice took advantage of her availability. By setting up her community service project as an opportunity for all students, Kyla felt that she helped Latrice maintain some dignity while getting needed academic assistance.

Social Action in the Classroom

The community service experiences that the prospective teachers had provoked lots of ideas about how social action might occur in the classroom.

Students Versus a Pizza Chain

In Robin's class the students were concerned about the school district's patronage of a local pizza chain that was part of a larger corporation with ties to a repressive regime in Asia. Robin's students were considering a soda pop boycott when they learned the company also owned the pizza chain.

The pizza chain prepared pizza once a month for each of the district's elementary schools. Pizza day was a big deal for the students, and the schools typically did the lunch count the day before to determine how many children would be eating pizza. Although many middle-income students rarely ate school lunches, pizza day was the exception; almost 100 percent of the students participated. Robin's students were faced with an ethical dilemma when they learned that the pizza they loved was a part of the corporation they had targeted for the boycott.

"Well, what do you want to do?" Robin asked the students. The students discussed a variety of options. Some students wanted to participate in a boycott; others talked about liking the pizza and wondering whether or not it made any difference for them to boycott. Finally, the discussion focused on how to avoid the pizza and spread the word about the pizza chain. The students began a project design to inform the school district of their concerns and educate their fellow students at Hughes School. The students felt that the idea of pizza day was a good one but that the district needed to select a different pizza vendor—one without problematic corporate ties. The students also wanted to let the other students in the school know why they were changing vendors. Robin helped the students craft letters to the superintendent and the school board members; they made posters to put up throughout the corridors of their school. The posters read, "No [name of pizza chain]" with the universal "no" symbol (red circle with line through it) and "[name of pizza chain] supports oppression," and "[name of pizza chain] hurts human rights." The posters were hung throughout the school; slowly other students began asking what they meant. The students were more than happy to provide explanations for why they thought the pizza chain should not be at the school.

A Turn-Off-the-Television Activity

After Kyla's earlier experience with the recycling project, she was anxious to develop another project for her 2nd and 3rd graders. The national observance of "Turn Off the Television Week" was an opportunity for a new project. In addition to encouraging her students to turn off their televisions for a week, Kyla saw this as an opportunity to work with the students on critical media literacy; many of her students used the television as a verification of their position on issues. It was not uncommon for a student to say, "Well, I saw it on TV" and presume that made it true. Kyla wanted to help the students be more discerning about what they were viewing on television.

Kyla started out by asking the students to maintain a log detailing what else they did in the evenings while the television was turned off. Kyla also asked the students to construct two lists—one of the good things about television and the other of the bad things. On the "good" lists students included, for example, "television is fun" and "you can learn things." On the "bad" lists students wrote things like "it makes you lazy," "it fools you," "it keeps you from using your brain," and "it keeps you from playing with your friends."

Analyis of Commercials and Cartoons

Kyla also had the students analyze some commercials to determine what they were attempting to make the students think. These seven- and eight-year-olds had no trouble uncovering the subtle messages of the commercials. They maintained a lively discussion about what television tries to do and how important it is for people to be careful about the messages they see and hear on television.

While Kyla was leading the discussion, one of the African American girls asked, "Miss K., how come when they show you 'Jumpin' Ginny (a doll that tumbles), only the white doll tumbles?" Kyla clearly did not know what the girl was referring to. "What do you mean?" she asked. "Yeah, she's right," chimed in another African American student. "First they show the commercial with the white doll doing everything, and at the end when they tell you where to buy it they have a black doll standing there, too." Soon the other students—white, Latino, Asian American—were concurring.

All of the children realized that the doll was being marketed to white consumers and that the black doll was something of an afterthought to absolve the manufacturer from charges of discrimination. All of this was news to Kyla, and it gave her some important insights into the students' perceptions about race relations. The students decided to write letters to the toy manufacturer to ask why the commercial was so one-sided. They also decided to monitor other commercials for examples of racism, sexism, and other forms of discrimination.

Kyla also showed the students segments from a television cartoon show that, like all cartoons, showed characters doing superhuman things. For example, a cartoon character survived after an anvil fell on his head and he was then run over by a truck. The students felt that the cartoons were funny but that they could confuse very young children.

As Kyla was about to wrap up the discussion, one of the students asked, "Miss K., if this is Turn-off-the-TV-Week, how come we're using the TV to answer all of these questions?" Kyla grinned when she told the students that her whole dilemma in planning the lesson had been just that. Finally, a student said, "I guess that's one of those good-bad things about television."

TFD Master's Projects

One requirement of the TFD program is the completion of a master's paper or project. Because of the intensity of the program we advised the students to work on projects that were closely tied to their teaching. We felt that it was easier for students to do master's papers or projects that would allow them to look carefully at their teaching rather than have them begin new projects while attempting to complete the certification requirements.

Bringing Values to Teaching

Most members of the Hughes cohort wrote master's papers[11] that examined their teaching and their commitment to social justice. Marcy wrote about the role of a student teacher in helping her students bridge the gap between their primary and secondary discourses. The presumptions on which she based her project were these:

- Many assessment tools, both formal and informal, must be used to gain a true understanding of a student, as well as his or her strengths and weaknesses.
- As a teacher I must be able to acknowledge my own preconceptions regarding my students so that I may avoid limiting my awareness of their strengths.
- I must also be willing to adapt to my students and take on different roles as I interact with them, carefully appraising

the effectiveness of these roles when used under different circumstances and with different students.

Near the end of her paper, Marcy quotes Delpit[12] when she says, "We do not really see through our eyes or hear through our ears, but through our beliefs." Tara decided to take on a new curriculum model the district was advocating. Rather than accept the next "fad" wholesale, she began an experiment in her class to see whether it was appropriate for meeting the educational needs of her diverse classroom. In her own words, Tara wrote, "In my actual practice as teacher, I discovered in order to improve upon my practice, I had to confront my culture and how it affected the spoken and unspoken truths about teaching."

As she grew through the reflective experience Tara wrote:

I bring these values to my teaching in ways I never realized. As a teacher, in order to motivate my students to succeed academically, I need to tap in on the core values which are part of their culture and learning. This is not something I understood in the beginning of my teaching. As a beginning practitioner, I was overwhelmed with the responsibility of management and control in my lesson. The knowledge was mine to teach, and in order to do this I had to have the upper hand in the experience. I was unwilling to share the power, and the result led to a struggle which was impossible to win.

Reflecting on Desegregation

Vanessa chose to do a critical review of the literature on school desegregation. She chose the topic because she had attended a town meeting in the city where people were arguing over whether or not to continue a pair-school desegregation effort.

Over the years many of the white families had left the elementary school in their community because African American children were bused to it. Vanessa wanted to buttress her own feelings about the issue with a thorough examination of the literature. In the introduction of her paper she wrote:

> Many of the parents present voiced their concerns and recommendations for the school system and what direction they felt the district needed to take. While listening to the audience members speak I began to reflect upon the issue raised by the report (concerning neighborhood versus busing to achieve desegregation). I had spent the majority of my education years in this "liberal" midwestern community. I remember the feelings of fear that I had moving from the south side of town, an area and school where I felt comfortable, to the east side of town, a place where I felt I did not fit in.

Using Drama in ESL Classes

Candy used her interest in drama to do a master's project with students receiving ESL services. She decided to do the project because she was concerned about the ways second language learners were being excluded from the teaching and learning in the classroom:

> As a teacher, I was concerned. Most of the children in the classroom were sitting on the carpet attentively watching me, waiting for my next instruction. . . . Two of the children in my class . . . were not only disengaged with the activity at hand, they sat away from the group, not interacting with anyone. . . . I recognized that they were not interested in the activity we were doing. . . . I was determined to engage these two children.

Teaching One Project Two Ways

Brenda focused her project on her attempt to teach a similar science unit on inventions to two different classes—a 1st grade class and a 2nd and 3rd grade class. She began the unit because she and Diana discovered that they were doing similar things in the integrated science class. What was striking about her project was her willingness to be self-critical:

> Even though I attempted to broaden the opportunities for all students to learn, I was not able to develop them with each student. I believe I may have let some of the students down by not attending to their learning styles and needs. . . . Perhaps I did not engage all of the students in the classroom. Maybe I did not give the students an environment that was supportive to encourage them to work at their own pace, to interact with others, be risk takers, or to generate confidence in themselves.

Brenda also focused on the tensions between the school curriculum and students' deeply held religious beliefs:

> In my journal I have written, "The topic of religion versus evolution came up today. I think I silenced Cassandra in my efforts to let all the students be heard. I'm sorry Cassandra." In my efforts to include both sets of beliefs and feelings, I failed to give either the time it deserved. I was trying not to show my view and trying to show that both sides have a right to be heard. My fear was by not presenting my view, I increased the focus on the opposite view and in so doing, I may have silenced the student with views similar to my own, that is, I may have made the student feel that her beliefs or feelings were not important or did not matter to the class discussion. I

felt I was balancing a tightwire between the religion and the scientific-evolution theories. In my attempt at trying to remain neutral, I ultimately endorsed the views that were the opposite of my own.

Rethinking Intelligence

Diana took on a project that was a challenge to the perspectives expressed by Herrnstein and Murray in *The Bell Curve*[13] and asked questions about our fundamental assumptions about intelligence as a construct. She set out to demonstrate that the students in class were smart in a variety of ways. She felt that her children, who represented African American, Hmong, Chinese, Latino, American Indian, and Filipino cultures, were a wonderful example of the different ways that human beings make sense of their world.

> [Gardner's] notion of multiple intelligences has given me a new way to look at students and at how to teach for the students I see. . . . The most important element of teaching is to find out who one's students are, to create a relationship based on mutual respect, and to foster this respect by providing opportunities for students to succeed. Neil had many opportunities to succeed in our classroom because most of the activities that we did in the room were ones in which he was interested. Stacy was successful in our room for the first half of the year, then began to refuse to work. My cooperating teacher and I worked really hard to try to re-engage Stacy in the curriculum. It wasn't until I really thought about why she might be refusing to work, and what she might respond positively to, that we began to rebuild a relationship.

Learning from the Students

Kyla wrote about her experiences with the various units she taught (for example, the recycling and AIDS units):

> I wrote this [master's] paper to reflect on—and argue for—high-interest, culturally relevant, and action-oriented curriculum, the greatest lesson I took away from the year with my cooperating teacher at Hughes School. As I began to understand and define for myself what engages and energizes students, I felt myself gaining the confidence and acuity critical for being a teacher for *all* learners. Had I completed my student teaching with the garbage and recycling unit, I would not have deemed myself a failure. But how would I have explained those lessons that I knew rang hollow and lacked energy? My year with Latrice transformed how I approached curriculum and children, particularly those children who had not been successful, academically and behaviorally.

Using New Lenses

Robin used her community service experience as the basis for her master's paper. However, she focused on the "Western bias" she brought to working with the southeast Asian student, Kenny:

> It is not easy to create a picture of Kenny because I found that so many of my early impressions of him—and even throughout my work with him—I was using decidedly "Western" definitions. This "Western" philosophy toward education I was employing was evident in my use of psychological explanations and tests to define his "deficits," my quickness in categorizing him and deciding what "level" he should be, my ideas

of what a child should be, my interpretation of his "behavior," and what I thought was a "lack" of emotion or assertiveness. . . . Although I felt I was "helping" Kenny to the best of my ability, what was my vision of childhood and learning for him? I remember feeling intense pressure that I was his only hope—that if I didn't "rescue"[14] him, his future was bleak. I gave him no credit for his own success.

Robin ended her paper with a quote from Asa Hilliard[15] that reflects purpose and reward of the community service aspect of the program: "Just as there is a vast untapped potential, yes, genius among the children, there is also a vast untapped potential among the teachers who serve the children. . . . Teachers need their own intellectual and emotional hunger to be fed. They need to experience the joy of collaborative discussion, dialogue, critique, and research."

Indicators of Sociopolitical Consciousness

Teaching with a sociopolitical consciousness is not easy. It requires teachers to incorporate the required curriculum and associated academic responsibilities with issues of social justice. Unfortunately, many teachers in urban schools are required to teach using scripts that tell them exactly what to teach and how to teach it.[16]

Indicators of teaching that promotes sociopolitical consciousness include the following:

- The teacher knows the larger sociopolitical context of the school-community-nation-world.
- The teacher has an investment in the public good.
- The teacher plans and implements academic experiences that connect students to the larger social context.

- The teacher believes that students' success has consequences for his or her own quality of life.

- *The teacher knows the larger sociopolitical context of the school-community-nation-world.* It is not unusual to hear reports of how little our teachers know. These reports usually focus on traditional facts, such as knowing the difference between the U.S. Senate and the House or being able to explain the Pythagorean theorem. Certainly we want teachers to be competent in both general knowledge and the specific knowledge they teach. However, culturally relevant teachers must have additional knowledge. They must have knowledge of the social and political realities in which they live. This means that they must expose themselves to a range of ideas beyond what appears in the daily newspaper and commercial television.

- *The teacher has an investment in the public good.* Culturally relevant teachers do what they do because they have a sense of the public good and a desire to participate in the civic culture. Despite the increasing privatization of goods and services, culturally relevant teachers understand that democracy is fragile and requires constant attention. Culturally relevant teachers are people who take the long view. The students in their classrooms are important for who they are *and* for who they can be.

- *The teacher plans and implements academic experiences that connect students to the larger social context.* As previously stated, culturally relevant teachers have to meet state and local curriculum requirements just like other teachers. However, because of their commitment to social justice and the public good, they are compelled to integrate their social commitment into the academic skills and knowledge of the curriculum. Even when the curriculum materials are limited, culturally relevant teachers know how to mine them to stimulate students' thinking and their learning of critical skills.

• *The teacher believes that students' success has consequences for his or her own quality of life.* Part of seeing students both as they are and how they can be involves maintaining a vision of how students' lives are integrally linked with the teacher. Far too often students of color have relayed at least one experience where a teacher has said something like, "It's up to you if you learn, and if you don't it doesn't matter to me. I'm still going to get paid" or "You're just cheating yourself. I've got mine; you've got yours to get." This notion that student learning is unconnected to the teacher is prevalent in classrooms where students are failing. The stance of culturally relevant teachers is that what happens to students ultimately happens to me. If students fail and are unable to be productive in society, then the cause of justice is not served. This means that the quality of life is diminished for everyone. Culturally relevant teachers' stakes in the society require an investment in the students' futures because it is the best way to ensure their own future.

The final chapter of the book points toward the promises and pitfalls of teacher education reform. It examines some of the current reform efforts and proposes some alternate views of preparing teachers to teach in diverse classrooms.

6

A Vision of the Promised Land

> We've got some difficult days ahead . . . and
> I may not get there with you . . . but I've
> been to the mountain top and I've seen the
> promised land.
>
> —*Martin Luther King Jr.*[1]

I stared at the list of requirements for teacher education. It was a dizzying array of professional courses and state requirements. I couldn't figure out how any of them fit with my goal to be a teacher. They were just another set of hurdles to be overcome. As I made my way through the courses it seemed that even on my small, historically black college campus the education professors were not talking to each other. Our assignments went from being remarkably similar to amazingly disparate. Many of the issues raised in the social foundation course were provocative, but we dealt with them solely in the abstract. Often the methods course required us to do an activity, but there was no discussion of the underlying concept or theory. One of my most enduring memories of my final year of school was me sprawled out on the floor trying to finish my "unit" before going out to a party. I was developing this unit for a set of students who did not yet exist for me. Why was I supposed to care what they learned?

Criticisms of Teacher Education

Teacher education has taken its share of criticism during this era of education reform, much of which is justified.

Students are required to take a series of courses that often have little relation to each other or the work of teaching. The field itself is regulated by state legislatures that allow politics to determine its direction. Even when the state and other agencies have pure motives regarding teacher education, the random assignment of requirements creates a hodgepodge of courses and workshops. The result is a dishonoring of the profession and a diminishing of the people in it.

The typical teacher education program requires students to take approximately two years of general education courses that are distributed across the humanities, social sciences, mathematics, natural sciences, and fine arts. By the junior year prospective teachers begin the professional education sequence. This sequence includes an introductory course, foundations courses in educational psychology and sociology, methods courses, and field experiences. There is nothing inherently good or bad about this arrangement. We know that teacher education does make a difference in teacher quality.[2] Students who attend high-performing schools are almost always taught by teachers who have completed a teacher education program. Students in our nation's poorest schools are more likely to be taught by people who are not certified teachers.

Use of Leverage Points

What would a teacher education program look like that was designed to serve diverse students who have struggled to learn? I argue that the actual names and content of the courses may not be as important as the program leverage points—places in the preparation of teachers where faculty and staff can make decisions about who can proceed toward certification. The most obvious leverage points are recruitment, pre-student teaching, and post-student teaching. Of course, one might argue that any place along the road to preparation could be a place to make decisions; indeed, when emergencies occur we do.

I once had a student in my practicum course who called to tell me that he did not think he would be able to do the nine-week practicum. His reason for doubting his ability to complete the practicum was that he needed "to eat a lot, to go to the bathroom a lot, and to smoke." I informed him that under no circumstances could he smoke in the school (all of our public schools are smoke-free). I then asked whether he had medical reasons for needing to eat and use the bathroom more than the allotted breaks during the day. He explained that he had no medical reasons; he just was accustomed to doing those things. I was emphatic that he could not. He indicated that he understood. Within a week after beginning the practicum I learned that he had become angry with a student and tripped him. I immediately removed him from the practicum and the program. He would not be a teacher on my watch.

But many problematic teacher certification decisions are not as clear-cut as this one. Such decisions often involve differences of opinions among the parties responsible for supporting students through the certification process. The supervisor and cooperating teacher may disagree. An adviser and a supervisor may disagree. The student and the cooperating teacher may disagree. The most often-used remedy for such disagreements is more time. We extend a practicum or field experience to give students a chance to demonstrate their competence. I once had a student who was minimally competent in the classroom, but she seemed to have almost no effect. I do not know whether she was depressed or her personality was just subdued, but her deadpan

manner made it difficult for her to manage a classroom. We ultimately recommended that she take some acting classes. We
could not dismiss her from teaching simply because she was
not perky.

Recruitment

When we make a decision to allow someone into a teacher prepa-
ration program, we almost guarantee that person's certification.
Some states require that admission into a teacher preparation program be contingent on attaining a passing score on a basic competency test. In California it is the California Basic Skills Test
(CBEST); in Wisconsin it is the Pre-Professional Skills
Test (PPST); in many states throughout the nation it is the
PRAXIS: Professional Assessment for Beginning Teachers exam.
I do think that determining a prospective teacher's basic competency is important. However, I think knowing that people are
"basically competent" is a very weak proxy for determining
whether or not they should be teachers.

Teaching in the more challenging schools requires maturity
and commitment to the public good. We have to do a better job
of seeing past the students' missionary zeal to "help those poor
children" and uncovering the talents of students who themselves
may have struggled to succeed in school. In my own university
I serve as a member of the athletic board. As an avowed sports
junkie, my role on the board gives me an opportunity to see athletes up close. I have seen scores of young people who have overcome incredible odds to attend a competitive, major university
and compete in a Division I sports program. Many of those students were good teacher candidates. However, the state and
institutional demands of our teacher education program prohib-
ited most of them from pursuing a career as a teacher.

During my time as a supervisor for TFD I ran into a young man who was volunteering at Hughes School. He was a former university football player and a reserve player for a professional football team. This meant that he had a year-to-year contract with the team and had to compete for a spot on the team each year. He did not know how long his career in professional football would last. As I watched him interacting with the students at Hughes, I could see that he had excellent rapport with them; he had the potential to be a good teacher. In one of our conversations he said that he wanted to be a teacher after his football career ended. When I asked whether he had considered teaching when he was an undergraduate, he told me that he was forced to choose between football and the many requirements of the teacher education program. He was a scholarship athlete, and football paid his bills. He did not have much of a choice.

In an ideal situation, teacher educators would interview prospective teachers before they enter a program. Haberman's[3] urban education program relies on a stringent interview protocol that attempts to determine students' ability to persist. Haberman insists that persistence is one of the primary qualities one seeks in an urban teacher. My interest in interviewing prospective teachers for teaching diverse students is in determining what life experiences they have that prepare them for this challenge.

Another reason I think it is important to interview students, particularly in a cohort program, is that teacher educators should attempt to *build* a cohort, not just accept those who meet admission criteria. Building a cohort means deciding the size and characteristics of the cohort. We need to determine the balance of gender, race, ethnicity, regional origin, and language ability we want in the program. We do not want to continue to graduate only women or only white students from elementary education programs.

In one of our TFD cohorts a student who was visually impaired completed the program. She was an outstanding teacher, and she helped her fellow cohort members think differently about what it means to be disabled. It did not mean she was "unable." It meant that she needed particular modifications in order to be successful.

Interviewing prospective teacher education candidates during recruitment also helps illuminate what the paper files represent. A student with a low grade point average one semester may have experienced something traumatic that semester. A student with a mediocre grade point average may have had to work full-time to pay for her college education. A student with a less-than-impressive grade point average may have challenged himself by taking many rigorous courses rather than courses in which he would be assured high grades. The interview is a place to determine the meaning of the files.

Pre–Student Teaching

Another leverage point is the time immediately before students are permitted to student teach. Because student teaching is a legal designation in most states, teacher education programs can be more stringent in determining who should continue. In some states student teachers have to be fingerprinted and pass a physical exam. It is not too difficult to demand that teacher educators "certify" that prospective teachers are ready to student teach. The general presumption is that if students have gotten that far, then they are ready to student teach. However, simply staying in the program provides no such assurance. Some programs are so large that it is difficult to say with certainty whether faculty and staff really know how prepared students are for student teaching.

Although I do not want to endorse the medical model as the appropriate paradigm for teaching, something of value is represented by the way medical school graduates seek their internships. Instead of ensuring students a placement, the pre-student teaching period could be one in which students vie for field experiences. Students would have to demonstrate that they have the appropriate skills for working in diverse class-rooms.

Once again, it might be important to interview students prior to sending them out to student teach. How much growth has a student demonstrated since the first interview? How have the student's ideas about teaching changed? What specific skills does the student believe she has? What specific skill does the student want to cultivate during the student teaching experience? At my university we allow the students in our regular elementary education program to observe the classrooms and interview the cooperating teacher in a class they are considering. The cooperating teachers rarely "interview" the prospective student teachers.

Post–Student Teaching

The folk wisdom about teacher education is that if you last until the end of the program, you will get your credential. Typically, only students who fail miserably leave the teacher education program without receiving their certification. Failing miserably means not attending, not being prepared, and not performing. Certification does not tell a school district whether or not someone is an excellent, mediocre, or marginal beginning teacher. Personnel officers and school principals must depend on sometimes-cryptic letters of recommendation to determine whether or not a new teacher will work out.

One way to assert more leverage would be to hold beginning teachers' certificates for a year. School districts would be permitted to hire teachers with the understanding that the first year is a supervised residency and that administrators, colleagues, and university faculty and staff will make an assessment of whether or not a beginning teacher should be fully certified at the end of the first full year of solo teaching. Each of the leverage points I discussed can provide teacher educators with important information about the quality of candidates. They require more labor, but they are not impossible to manage. They probably mean that we need to consider smaller programs in which teacher candidates can be closely monitored. Each of these leverage points figures into my vision for an excellent teacher education program.

A Vision: The Urban Teacher Academy

Despite having spent more than thirty years teaching, I still dream about improving the education of teachers. My mythical Urban Teacher Academy (UTA) contains elements of programs I have both seen and read about. It also contains elements high on my wish list for teacher education.

UTA is located in a major urban university; it is affiliated with a small number of urban schools that are committed to working with the university. UTA is a competitive program that admits twenty to twenty-five students each year. Admission into UTA guarantees the candidates tuition, a stipend, and a job.

UTA Values

UTA is dedicated to principles of diversity and reflects that in its faculty and staff. Each year it builds a cohort of diverse teacher candidates—African American, Latino and Latina,

Asian American, American Indian, and European American. Prospective candidates already possess an undergraduate degree. Preference is given to students who have taken more rigorous courses in the humanities, sciences, social sciences, mathematics, or the arts.

Preference is also given to students who speak a second language other than English. All students must pass a second language proficiency test before completing their certificate. The faculty that teaches in UTA also reflects a high degree of diversity. Faculty members have experience in urban communities, facility in several languages, and ongoing ties to the community through teaching, service, and research.

UTA Partnerships and Placements

During the first year of UTA, teacher candidates form a partnership with one or more service agencies in the community. Some candidates partner with local churches; some partner with the neighborhood health center; some partner with preschool and child-care agencies. A few candidates arrange their own unique partnerships based on specific skills or needs they perceive. Teacher candidates work with the partnership agencies or individuals for ten hours each week. Students participate in a weekly seminar to discuss what they are learning and what questions they are developing about the community because of their partnership experiences.

During the first summer, UTA teacher candidates are placed with a family in the school community. The placements are made through the local churches and community agencies. The home placements provide the UTA teacher candidates with their best opportunity to know the people and their cultures. The summer placement lasts for six weeks, and UTA students are expected to function as family members, not guests or teachers. They do their share of household chores and share in typical family activities.

The UTA Program

In the fall UTA students spend their mornings observing and assisting in the classroom. In the afternoons they take courses leading toward certification. The courses are offered at the school site and take advantage of the availability of experienced teachers to participate in the courses.

During this semester UTA students begin assembling their teaching portfolios. The portfolio contains examples of reflective papers and curriculum projects, as well as evidence of teaching progress. The portfolio also contains testimonials from experienced teachers, parents, and community members. These testimonials can be in the form of written documents, personal interviews, videotapes, or audiotapes. The portfolio serves as one aspect of the prospective teachers' assessment.

During this first year the UTA students are observed once a week. The supervisor provides the prospective teacher with feedback about his or her progress. At the end of the semester each UTA student makes a presentation before a panel of university faculty, inservice teachers, administrators, and community members. In the presentation the UTA student argues her case as to why she should continue in the program. The UTA student describes what she has learned thus far in the program and presents a plan for what she hopes to learn in the upcoming semester. The panel decides whether or not the UTA student should proceed to the second semester, repeat the first semester assignment, or discontinue in the program.

The second semester is similar to the first except that students are required to take on additional teaching responsibilities. Once again, the semester ends with a panel presentation. At this presentation the panel decides whether or not to recommend the UTA student for a provisional teaching certificate that allows the student to teach in one of the UTA schools. Teachers can continue in their training school or switch to another UTA school. To secure a position in a UTA school, provisional teachers must interview with the school principal, staff, and community members. Most provisional teachers prefer to remain at their "training" schools, but that placement is not guaranteed. UTA provisional teachers who do change schools must develop and implement a plan for getting to know their new school community.

Quarterly Meetings

A UTA provisional teacher is assigned a class that is smaller than usual (ten to twelve students) and receives 80 percent of a first-year teacher's salary, along with full benefits. A lead or mentor teacher is assigned to function as on-site supervisor for the provisional teacher. Provisional teachers are required to schedule four meetings per year with the school principal and their university supervisor. The meetings are designed to help the provisional teacher begin to map out his or her career path. Rather than assume that all new teachers will spend their entire careers in the classroom, the UTA program promotes a teaching career path. Does the new teacher envision herself as a principal someday? Does the new teacher think that being a reading teacher or counselor would be fulfilling?

The quarterly meetings are also designed to help provisional teachers select appropriate professional development activities. Instead of attending one-size-fits-all "inservice days," the UTA program believes that teachers must be more involved in shaping their own professional and career development paths. Some teachers select more traditional paths and work toward completing an advanced degree; others choose more innovative strategies for fulfilling professional development goals. For example, some teachers may be interested in becoming more active in professional associations. Those teachers select membership in a professional association and attendance at national or regional association meetings as a part of their professional development. Part of their responsibility in the school community is to share information about curriculum and teaching with their colleagues.

The quarterly meetings also are used for providing feedback to the provisional teacher. The mentor teacher provides documentation of teaching observations, and the provisional teacher continues to maintain a teaching portfolio. The provisional teachers also work on one presentation or workshop they will deliver at an end-of-the-year conference sponsored by the university. The audience for the conference includes their teacher colleagues, teacher educators, and UTA students who are in the first year of preparation.

Another aspect of the quarterly meeting focuses on student learning. The provisional teacher must present a detailed plan for ensuring the academic success of each of the students in her class. The plan must identify where students began academically and where the teacher hopes to move the students; it must document progress along the way. The student learning plan is a way to help new teachers remember that their primary responsibility is to support the academic achievement of each student. Maintaining a small class size allows the teacher to know each student well.

Finally, after four successful quarterly meetings the UTA provisional teacher can earn her first-level teaching certificate. This certificate becomes a second-level (or tenured) teaching certificate after the first-level teacher completes state and district requirements for tenure. A provisional teacher who has one "unsatisfactory" quarterly meeting has his or her provisional teaching extended for a half year. A provisional teacher who has two unsatisfactory quarterly meetings is asked to leave the program.

As is evident by the UTA, teacher educators can take maximum advantage of various leverage points throughout the teacher preparation program. Instead of working to maintain students in a program at all cost, UTA seeks to ensure that the prospective teachers it prepares are appropriate for urban classrooms filled with students of various races, ethnic groups, and language groups.

What We Learned from TFD

After the third cohort of students completed TFD, I must admit that my colleagues and I breathed a sigh of relief. We were happy not to be trying to juggle an incoming and outgoing cohort during the summer. We were ecstatic about not having to do another round of master's exams throughout the summer. We were overjoyed at the prospect of not running seminars each semester, supervising student teachers, and writing piles of letters of recommendations. We were delighted at the idea of returning to overdue commitments we had made to writing and research. But we did learn from our participation in TFD, and those lessons inform our ongoing work with teachers and teacher educators. Here is some of what we learned:

Prospective teachers working in diverse communities need the chance to learn about the students in the context of the community.

Many years ago a teacher colleague told me, "School is the worst place to try to learn something." She was referring to her penchant for taking her students on field trips and other out-of-the-classroom experiences. But her words rang true for me throughout TFD. School is typically the first place that most children encounter failure. Students' success at home and in the community rarely reflects itself in school tasks. By placing our TFD students in community-based programs (for example, day camps, neighborhood centers, community-run activities) the TFD students came to form different opinions about students' strengths and capabilities.

Prospective teachers working in diverse community schools need an opportunity to apprentice with skilled cooperating teachers.

We considered the student teaching year an apprenticeship year rather than a "performance" year. Although the notion of apprenticeship does not precisely explain the work of TFD students, it comes closer than other terms I could imagine. It was not an internship because internships typically represent the work of people who have already experienced some training and have attempted to put that training to use in a supervised setting. The students were not engaged in the typical student teaching because their responsibilities were greater than typical student teachers, and they were not asked to "perform" the lessons they learned in their methods courses. Rather, their placement with knowledgeable, skilled, experienced teachers gave them the opportunity to try new things in a context of supportive critique.

Prospective teachers working in diverse school communities need an opportunity to ask lots of questions about teachers and teaching.

In most forms of professional practice, novices are encouraged and expected to ask questions about their work. Medical interns, law clerks, and cub reporters all understand that the way to improve their skills and earn a place in their respective fields is to ask insightful questions to enhance their professional repertoires. Because the TFD students were not expected to perform in front of the class, they came in filled with questions about students, the classroom, the school, and the community.

Prospective teachers need the opportunity to do serious intellectual work.

Perhaps it comes from the persistence of Hollywood images of teachers in our culture, but most people do not believe that teachers do intellectual work. Michele Pfeiffer in the movie *Dangerous Minds*, Edward James Olmos in *Stand and Deliver*, and Robin Williams in *The Dead Poet's Society* are examples of the images of teachers that are inscribed in the public mind. They are heroic, selfless, compassionate, super humans who barge into drug-infested and dangerous communities, rescue children from their "pitiful" circumstances, and make students' worlds safe for them. However, such depictions on the silver screen rarely show the intellectual work of teaching. Hollywood teachers do not prepare lessons; neither do they take graduate courses or participate in professional networks.

What we attempted to do with the TFD participants was make sure they understood that intellectual work was a major part of the enterprise. We challenged them to use theory (test it, challenge it, reinvent it) as they improved their practice. Although we were concerned about how they felt about aspects of their work, we perhaps were more concerned about how they *thought* about their work.

We also learned that a program like TFD cannot deal with all of the challenges prospective teachers face. Such programs also cannot overcome the limitations of institutions like schools, universities, and state departments of education. Despite the excellent people we recruited into the program, we continued to struggle with helping them become well-prepared beginning teachers. We recognized that some of our students lacked an appreciation for the complexity of teaching.

In the first year of the program eight of the twenty-five TFD students left the program before earning their teaching certification. Some thought that as long as they knew enough subject matter, students would be compliant and receptive. Before long they understood that teaching is a demanding and stressful job. The responsibilities of teaching extend beyond teacher and student; they include parents, communities, colleagues, and supervisors. All of these various constituencies are important.

Our students struggled to translate complex social issues into meaningful curriculum. Teacher educators can harp on the need for prospective teachers to engage students in social justice concerns, but those concerns must remain age-appropriate. Those concerns must help students use their intellectual skills to wrestle with powerful ideas and complex issues. One of our TFD students wanted the 2nd and 3rd grade students she was teaching to understand human rights issues facing people in various parts of Asia. However, the students did not understand enough geography to be able to understand where their concerns should be directed. The students did not know enough about the culture to be able to understand other interpretations of the situation. And the students did not know enough about issues of rights to act or respond beyond their personal feelings. Issues involving racism, gender discrimination, sexuality, and class privilege require teachers to both know the issues and how children learn.[4]

We deliberately chose students for TFD who did express interest in social justice and diversity issues. We deliberately chose students whose personal experiences and life choices caused them to confront social justice issues. However, some of our students were ideologues who did not (or would not) understand that school interactions are delicate dances of compromise. No matter what one's personal philosophy may be, one is likely to encounter students in a classroom who hold opposing philosophies. One of our prospective teachers was a vegetarian. Her commitment to not eating meat was tied to her participation in animal rights activities. When her students talked about family meal activities—barbecues, Thanksgiving dinner, Sunday brunches—the prospective teacher wrinkled her nose and talked about how wrong it was to eat animals. The students were visibly shaken by her anti-meat "lectures" and felt she was acting irresponsibly. The prospective teacher did not complete our program.

Most of the prospective teachers in our program could organize lessons that were appropriate for the children they taught. Most did not impose their personal philosophies and viewpoints on their students. However, a number had more common pedagogical concerns. For instance, some of our prospective teachers seemed overly concerned with issues of classroom order and discipline, probably stemming from many places. Novice teachers may take order and discipline as indicators of their own competence. Conversely, they read lax classroom order and discipline as personal incompetence.

At the opposite end of the spectrum, some of our prospective teachers seemed to exhibit a lack of regard for a sense of classroom order and discipline. In their attempt to be democratic and nonhierarchical they allowed the children to make decisions they were unprepared to make. The prospective teachers' democracies were turning into anarchy, and their understanding of a teacher's power and authority was distorted.

Other aspects of our learning as teacher educators were related less to what our prospective teachers were doing and more to what we were doing programmatically. For example, the TFD program was too intense—almost to the detriment of critical and reflective practice. We scheduled every available time slot from early morning to late afternoon. By the time our prospective teachers left for the day, took care of their own needs, and began planning for the next day (for example, completing lesson plans and homework), they were too tired to reflect on their practice. Keeping their journals became more of a chore than a way to develop personally and professionally.

We also recognized that our program contained holes. In particular, we did not pay enough attention to issues of second-language acquisition and research methodology. Even in a mid-sized, midwestern city like ours, second-language learners were becoming an increasing proportion of our school population. Our program provided prospective students little in the way of understanding language acquisition and language processes. We also failed to provide the students with enough preparation and training in research methodology. As participants in a master's-level program our students were required to complete a master's paper or project. Unlike our traditional master's program students, they had no space in their schedules to take courses on research design and quantitative and qualitative methods. We benefited from the fact that our students were extremely bright and able to read and conduct research well on their own. By the second year's cohort the faculty worked more closely with the students to develop action research papers or portfolio projects that were more representative of master's-level work.

Finally, our program failed to provide the level of professional development for our cooperating teachers that we had hoped for. In our original plan we wanted the cooperating teachers to be actively involved in planning and designing the methods courses and the field experience seminars. Initially, cooperating teachers were active participants in making suggestions for and reviewing course syllabi. We talked about maintaining electronic conversations and course updates. We also wanted cooperating teachers to be active in deciding how the TFD students would be used in their schools and communities. We wanted the seminars to be places where cooperating teachers felt welcome to come to share expertise and learn.

Once the school year began those lofty goals became harder to attain. Cooperating teachers still had classrooms of children and their families to attend to. They still had the burden of nurturing budding professionals. Their own professional learning seemed to slip further and further down their list of priorities. Teachers were reluctant to make administrative decisions about student-teacher placements and assignments. Teachers had little time or opportunity to keep up with the methods courses and seminars. We also learned that our prospective teachers felt more comfortable when their seminars occurred away from their school sites. Although we had no evidence that teachers were "eavesdropping" on the seminars, some TFD students told us that they felt more guarded and constrained about talking at the school site. For them, the university provided a safe space to share their ideas and express concerns.

Even with its shortcomings, TFD offers some promise for thinking creatively about teacher education. Our early stumbles can serve as future stepping stones. Some of its components are firmly placed in my mythical UTA. Teacher education cannot reform itself by itself. It needs help from constituents across the educational landscape. It also needs help from an undervalued source—novice teachers. Those of us who work in teacher education may see some incremental changes in the field, but we are unlikely to see and participate in a "promised land" of teaching and learning. That joy is reserved for those new to the profession. Like the ancient Hebrew leader Moses, we are charged with the responsibility of liberating the field from the enslavement of narrow thinking about curriculum and human capacity. However, we will not enjoy the direct benefits of that struggle. Those benefits are to accrue to a new generation of leadership—a generation that will cross over to Canaan.

Appendix A: Methodology

The interest of some who read this volume is in how the study was conducted and how it might be replicated. *Crossing Over to Canaan* describes a qualitative, ethnographic study in which the researcher functioned as a participant-observer. This appendix describes the rationale for the study and the research design.

Why Study Teacher Education?

Teacher education is a practice that goes on in thousands of places throughout the nation and the world. Because it is grounded in practice and is labor-intensive, it may seem like doing double duty to study it. However, the constant assault on public education and teachers, in particular, demands that we produce well-conceived, careful studies of the practice of teachers and teacher educators.

My rationale for studying this particular program (Teach for Diversity) was to provide my colleagues and myself information as we move toward changes in our overall program. The study also gave me an opportunity to test a previously proposed theory of culturally relevant education.[1]

Theoretical Framework

The theory that guided this work is one I developed from working with experienced teachers who were successful teachers of African American students. I call this theory *culturally relevant pedagogy*. It is based on three propositions about what contributes to success for all students, especially African American students. These propositions are

- Successful teachers focus on students' academic achievement.
- Successful teachers develop students' cultural competence.
- Successful teachers foster students' sense of sociopolitical consciousness.

I used this theoretical framework to ask questions about the role of teacher preparation in helping teachers become more effective in diverse classrooms. The specific research questions that guided my inquiry were as follows:

What is the role of teacher education in preparing teachers for diverse classrooms?

What is the role of teacher background in ensuring teacher effectiveness in diverse classrooms?

What is the process of change experienced by teachers who decide to work in diverse classrooms?

Research Design

This study was a qualitative, year-long ethnographic study of eight novice teachers as they completed an experimental teacher education program. The sample comprised new teachers with an expressed desire to teach in schools serving students from diverse cultural, ethnic, linguistic, and ability groups.

The participants acted as coconstructors of the knowledge for this project, agreeing that all aspects of their learning to become teachers were available for analysis and review. Thus, I collected data from multiple sources: initial statements of interest, participant observations of classrooms, lesson plans, seminar notes, master's papers or projects, and ethnographic interviews.[2]

The initial statements of interest were a part of each TFD applicant's file. Because I did not know which students would be chosen, the statements were not preselected. After the cohort was determined, I was given permission to retrieve the initial statements. I analyzed these statements to determine the novice teachers' attitudes about diversity and the prospect of teaching students different from themselves. The initial statements were also important comparison documents at the end of the program to determine what ways, if any, participating in TFD affected the teachers' beliefs and attitudes.

My role as a supervisor in the program automatically made me a participant in the development of the novice teachers' practices. The issue of researcher subjectivity came to the fore in this project. I was not merely a passive observer of novice teachers struggling to learn to teach, but I was also responsible for developing and evaluating that teaching. What I have to say about the teachers is therefore as much about me as it is about the teachers and the program.

This comingling of roles is a common occurrence in anthropological fieldwork. It is rare for a community to allow someone to merely "watch" them go about their work and their daily lives. The "watcher" must also work. The ethnographies edited by George and Louise Spindler[3] often detail the way researchers become integrated into a community. I did not attempt to disentangle my role as supervisor from that of researcher. Rather, I attempted to treat all aspects of the supervision as portions of data. For instance, my observations were recorded in much the same way I collect field notes. I maintained two-column logs; the left-hand column contained words, actions, and gestures the teacher made, and the right-hand column contained students' words, actions, and gestures. On the far left margin I recorded the time at five- to-seven-minute intervals. The observation logs contained no evaluation or interpretation of the teachers' or students' words, actions, or gestures.

At the end of the observation I shared what I had recorded on the log and asked a series of questions: "How close did the lesson resemble what you planned to do?" "What do you think worked well?" "What do you think did not work as well as you would have liked?" "How do you intend to follow this up?" I also asked the students if they wanted some suggestions. This last question was part of my "role-switch" from researcher to supervisor. Within twenty-four to forty-eight hours I wrote a summary of the observation with suggestions for improvement. These summaries did not become a part of the project's dataset because they contained my evaluation of the novice teachers' work.

The lesson plans were documents I consulted to determine what the teachers felt were important ideas, concepts, and skills to be taught. I did not use the lesson plans to evaluate teachers' practice, as novice teachers' lesson plans tend to be done to honor program requirements, not teaching requirements. However, the broad concepts of what people are attempting to teach and how they think about that teaching are apparent in the lesson plans.

The seminar notes were among the more valuable pieces of data I collected. The students participated in cohort seminars during fall and spring semesters. These seminars were intimate and participatory. My field notes again reflect their words, actions, and gestures. I use a stenographer's pad to collect field notes. The divided page provides the two columns I need—one for documenting what is transpiring and the other for making tentative interpretations and raising questions. For example, one field note entry looks like this: [left-hand column] "Tara says, 'one of my kids just hates math and I don't know how to get him to just try.' Candy looks disinterested." [right-hand column] "Perhaps Candy's struggle with Jimmy is making her think Tara's problem is insignificant. Check this out." There are thirty sets of seminar notes (one set for each week of each fifteen-week semester). However, they vary in quality and usefulness. Some are more procedural—course selection, information dissemination, form completion; others are more substantive.

The master's papers and projects provided a wealth of data. They reflect the novice teachers' intellectual interests and synthesis of what they garnered from the program and were able to apply to their teaching practice. The master's papers and projects offered so much information that I fear that what is shared here does not do justice to them. However, because they are "texts" authored by the teachers that stand alone, it would not be ethical for me to over-represent them in a text that bears my name. I used the papers and projects as a data source for those aspects of the theoretical framework described in the section mentioned earlier. Some of the richness of the data from the papers is necessarily lost in this newly reinterpreted text because the purposes of the students' papers and my text are different.

Finally, I conducted an ethnographic interview with each of the novice teachers at the end of the program. These interviews lasted from one and one-half to two and one-half hours. I conducted the interviews at a time and place the participants deemed most convenient and conducive. Some of the teachers requested that I conduct the interview at their homes. These interviews tended to be longer because they permitted more privacy, and the teachers felt free to go into more detail and reveal more personal anecdotes and feelings. All interviews were taped and transcribed; I also took notes. Although I asked each of the teachers the same set of questions, their responses dictated the type and number of follow-up or probing questions I asked. The general questions were as follows:

Let's start by having you say a bit about your own background—how you grew up, your own schooling experiences, and how you happen to come to this point.

Why did you decide to become a teacher?

What made you decide on the Teach for Diversity program?

What are some of the things that you think you've learned over the past fifteen months?

As you look at the program in general, what do you see as some of its strengths?

What do you think you got from the classes? The field experiences? The seminar? The supervision?

What do you see as some of the program's weaknesses?

As you look back over the year, can you think of a student with whom you seemed to relate especially well? Why do you think this was so?

Was there a youngster with whom you think you struggled the whole year? Why do you think this was so?

How do you think you've changed as a result of this year's experiences?

Is there anything else about the program you want to comment on?

Data Analysis

One of the more challenging aspects of qualitative research is data analysis. Studies of this type generate a huge amount of data that must be sorted and selected in ways that tell a coherent story. However, such selection cannot be done in ways that tell only stories that represent the researcher's point of view.

To work against over-representation of my personal perspectives I chose to enter all textual data into the NU*DIST/ NVIVO qualitative analysis software programs.[4] The broad themes I sought were those of culturally relevant pedagogy—academic achievement, culture and cultural competence, and sociopolitical consciousness, using a variety of synonyms for each of these concepts. The themes helped me locate the words or phrases, but I elected to then read the entire section to determine the context in which the themes emerged. The software was a valuable tool, but ultimately I relied on my own qualitative research skills to interpret and make sense of the thematic strands. Errors in interpretation are mine alone.

The Metaphor

Rather than refer to a Discussion or Results section, I chose to reference the overarching metaphor of this work. As I stated in the Preface, I saw the role of new teachers who choose to work in diverse classrooms as analogous to that of the biblical character Joshua. The new teachers in this text were already energetic and enthusiastic about teaching in diverse classrooms. They did not have to be convinced to do it or do it by default. They sought out a program that would make it possible for them to prepare and teach in these classrooms. Most of them continue to teach in such environments.[5]

The metaphor is also important because it signals the need for the education community to recognize the potential of novices in crafting a pedagogy that addresses some of the intractable challenges of educating students in and for a diverse society. The Sojourners represent a new iteration of novice teachers—unafraid to take on a challenge and unafraid to participate in a process of intellectual and personal transformation.

Appendix B:
The Teach for Diversity Program

Some readers will be more interested in the specific components of the Teach for Diversity (TFD) program than in the study methodology. This appendix is designed to share the program's philosophy and the sequence and description of courses for those who have responsibility for teacher education program direction, coordination, or implementation. The courses are listed by course title rather than by number because our numbering system means nothing beyond our campus. All courses are offered at the graduate level.

The TFD Philosophy

We advertised[1] the TFD program as a response to the growing number of school districts that are serving students from diverse backgrounds, even as the teaching population is increasingly white, monolingual, middle class, and female. We described the program as one whose curriculum "is integrated across disciplinary boundaries." We detailed the program expectations and admissions criteria this way:

> One expectation of the UW-Madison program is to prepare teachers who accept and promote access and equal opportunity for all students to the central areas of learning in the school and classroom, and who affirm educational equity with

curriculum, instruction, and schooling practices for students who are marginalized.

A second expectation of the program is that all graduate students will develop a keener awareness of their own multiple group memberships. Consequently, students can become knowledgeable about the multiple histories, ideas, and beliefs of all groups in U.S. society and how these are represented and omitted in curriculum.

A third expectation of the program is that students develop an understanding of teaching that will allow them to exercise "situational diversity," taking into account the home-school context in their choice of curriculum and teaching strategies.

A fourth expectation of the program is to provide a dedicated and knowledgeable teaching staff—university faculty, elementary school teachers and administrators, and community members—who will provide the structure and guidance in helping graduate students take responsibility for their own educational preparation for teaching for diversity.

One part of the admission process is to apply the set of criteria for admission to a master's degree program in our department, including

- An earned bachelor's degree
- A 3.00 undergraduate GPA in the last 60 credits (students with a lower GPA take the Graduate Records Examination)
- Submission of three letters of reference (two of which must be from academic sources)
- Pre-Professional Skills Test (PPST) scores, per Wisconsin Department of Public Instruction requirements
- Minimum GPA of 3.25 on completion of the program

In addition to these requirements for the master's degree and entry to a teacher certification program, applicants submit a two- or three-page written statement about their reasons for entering teaching, and about their academic, work, and personal background. A committee of university and public school faculty assesses these written materials and other admissions data and may interview the applicants who appear to be most qualified. Then a cohort group is constructed, taking into account individuals' strengths and the program's desire to have a multicultural learning community.

Program Courses

First Summer

General Seminar: Teaching and Diversity. This course is designed to help students consider the ways that notions of diversity are constructed. It is a theoretical course that helps students understand how diversity discourses are shaped and how their own conceptions of diversity and schooling will impact the way they approach teaching in settings that are likely to be different from their own experiences. The readings in this course deal with perspectives on race, class, gender, and language. Local school principals, teachers, and community activists visit the class to share their perspectives on issues of diversity and schooling.

Culture, Curriculum, and Learning. This course is designed to help students understand the intersections of culture (including language), curriculum, and learning. The course draws on the social sciences of anthropology, sociology, and psychology to assist students in recognizing the pervasive ways that culture impacts human endeavors. A major project in this course is the development of a mini-ethnography in which students attempt to explain the "deep structures" of a particular setting. The course includes speakers from practice—teachers, administrators, community-based agents, and agencies.

Summer Practicum. The Summer practicum is a field-based component of the program. The students are placed in a community agency that serves elementary-aged students (for example, day camp, summer learning program, recreation center). The reason for this experience is to begin to help prospective teachers mesh theory with practice. The practicum is accompanied by a weekly seminar where students begin to reflect on the process of interacting with children and learning to teach.

Fall

Health, Physical Education, and Social Studies. This is one of three "methods" courses in the program. Practicing teachers in conjunction with university faculty planned each of the methods courses. The course asks three central questions about who we are, how we interact with others, and how we take care of ourselves and our surroundings. The students are required to produce either a child study or an integrated thematic unit. Some students opt to do a modified version of both. The course is team taught by a social studies educator and a physical educator, with visits from experts in health-related fields.

Literacy and the Arts. This course represents an expanded notion of what has traditionally been considered "reading and language arts." In it students are exposed to major theories and conceptions about literacy, as well as new and innovative approaches to this area. Students enter the "literacy debate" and make sense of the daunting task of teaching children to read. The course is linked to the arts—music, visual arts, and

drama—as a way to develop expanded literacy for all students. Course requirements include the development of a text set, an artful interpretive project, and a journal to record literacy observations and interpretations.

Mathematics, Science, and Environmental Education. This course is an integration of mathematics and science. Two theories or concepts frame this course—Cognitively Guided Instruction (CGI) and Conceptual Change Theory.[2] Both of these ideas take a problem-centered approach to learning. Students are challenged to understand the ways that children's problem-solving abilities can be an impetus for developing mathematics and science curriculum. The course is team taught by a mathematics educator and a science educator.

Fall Practicum. The Fall practicum is a field-based experience designed to introduce students to the complexities of schooling in diverse communities. This practicum is limited to one of three diverse school sites that students remain in for the entire academic year. Prospective students spend three days (Wednesdays through Fridays) at their school sites. This practicum requires students to observe and assist in the classroom and gradually begin assuming limited teaching responsibilities. Practicum evaluation is determined in conjunction with the cooperating teacher and university supervisor. A weekly seminar accompanies the practicum where student-initiated issues are explored. Although they may vary, it is likely that issues such as classroom management, planning, assessment, and organization will surface. In addition to school-based experiences, each student is required to do ten hours of community service per week. This community service is linked to the students' practice. Typical community service projects include after-school tutoring, mentoring, assisting in a community or recreation center, conducting family-based education, and assisting social service agencies that provide food and shelter.

Spring

Inclusive Schooling. This is the first "general" course that TFD students experience. It is taken along with all regular program teacher education students. This course is state-mandated and deals with methods and strategies for including special needs students in regular education classrooms. The course is accompanied by a discussion section where students integrate their experiences and understanding from their practice with ideas and concepts from inclusive schooling. Because of the uniqueness of their experiences, the TFD students are assigned a separate discussion section.

Student Teaching. Students remain at their Fall practicum sites and begin a full semester of supervised student teaching. Student teaching requires that students assume more responsibility for the classroom and begin to implement some of the curriculum and strategies learned during Fall coursework. Each student is required to do at least two weeks of lead teaching; they assume responsibility for the entire classroom. The lead weeks are preceded by lead mornings and lead days. Lesson planning and long-range planning in student teaching is done with the assistance and approval of the cooperating teacher. Student teaching is accompanied by a weekly seminar.

Second Summer

Social Issues and Education. This course is an upper-division iteration of the undergraduate "School and Society" course. The course is offered by the Educational Policy Studies Department.

The course deals with the social influences on schooling. What are the social purposes of schooling? How does a society make priorities about education and schooling? What are the major issues and challenges facing contemporary schooling? The course allows students to reflect on their year of field experiences in relation to various social theories.

Human Development in Infancy and Early Childhood. This is the second "general" course that TFD students take with the regular teacher education program. It is a study of child development, designed to help students understand the psychological development of children. It covers topics such as cognitive development, personal and social development, individual differences, behaviorism, cognitivism, constructivism, motivation, exceptionality, learning, and instruction.

Research. Students enroll in research credits during the summer to complete their master's papers or projects. This work typically takes the form of action research, centered in their year-long practice, or an archival (library-based) study of an important educational issue or practice. The students need a committee of three faculty members to assist in this project. A master's exam (usually an oral defense of the paper) is required.

Notes

Introduction

1. Portions of this chapter were taken from Ladson-Billings, G. "Preparing Teachers for Diverse Student Populations: A Critical Race Theory Perspective." In A. Iran-Nejad and P. D. Pearson, (eds.). *Review of Research in Education, 24,* (pp. 211–247). Washington, D.C.: American Educational Research Association, 1999.

2. Farkas, S., Johnson, J. and Foleno, T. "A Sense of Calling: Who Teaches and Why." New York: Public Agenda, 2000.

3. Farkas, and others, 2000, p. 29.

4. Haberman, M. *Star Teachers of Children in Poverty.* West Lafayette, IN: Kappa Delta Pi, 1995.

5. Haberman, 1995, p. 4.

6. Ladson-Billings, 1999.

7. Delpit, L. *Other People's Children: Cultural Conflict in the Classroom.* New York: New Press, 1995.

8. American Association of Colleges of Teacher Education. Briefing books. Washington, D.C.: Author, 1994.

9. King, J. "Dysconscious Racism: Ideology, Identity and the Miseducation of Teachers." *Journal of Negro Education, 60,* 1991, 133–146.

10. Zimpher, N. and Ashburn, E. "Countering the Parochialism in Teacher Candidates." In M. Dilworth (ed.). *Diversity in Teacher Education* (pp.40-62). San Francisco: Jossey-Bass, 1992.

11. McWilliam, E. *In Broken Images: Feminist Tales for a Different Teacher Education*. New York: Teachers College Press.

12. Johnson, S. M. "Teaching's Next Generation." *Education Week, 19*(39), June 7, 2000, pp. 33, 48.

13. McNeil, L. "Creating New Inequalities: Contradictions of Reform." *Phi Delta Kappan, 81*, June 2000, 728–734.

14. See for example, the Holmes Group report "Teachers for Tomorrow's Schools" and the Carnegie report, "A Nation Prepared: Teachers for the Twenty-First Century."

15. Farkas and others, 2000, p. 29.

16. Farkas and others, 2000, p. 30.

Chapter One

1. See, for example, Grant, C. A. and Secada, W. "Preparing Teachers for Diversity." In W. R. Houston, M. Haberman, and J. Sikula (eds.), *Handbook of Research on Teacher Education* (pp. 403–422). New York: Macmillan, 1990; King, J. E., Hollins, E., and Hayman, W. (eds.). *Preparing Teachers for Cultural Diversity*. New York: Teachers College Press, 1997; Ladson-Billings, G. "Multicultural Teacher Education: Research, Practice, and Policy." In J. A. Banks and C. M. Banks (eds.), *Handbook of Research in Multicultural Education* (pp. 747–759). New York: Macmillan, 1995.

2. American Association of Colleges of Teacher Education. *Briefing Books*. Washington, D.C.: American Association of Colleges of Teacher Education, 1994.

3. Ladson-Billings, G. "Preparing Teachers for Diverse Student Populations: A Critical Race Theory Perspective." In A. Iran-Najed and P. D. Pearson (eds.), *Review of Research in Education, 24*. Washington, D.C.: American Educational Research Association, 1999.

4. Haberman, M. *Star Teachers of Children in Poverty*. Lafayette, Ind.: Kappa Delta Pi, 1995.

5. Haberman, 1995, p. 49.

6. National Commission on Teaching and America's Future. *What Matters Most: Teaching and America's Future*. New York: National Commission on Teaching and America's Future, 1996.

7. The novice teachers discussed in this book are given pseudonyms.

8. See the work of Zeichner, K., and Liston, D. "Traditions of Reform in U.S. Teacher Education." *Journal of Teacher Education*, 1990, *41*, 3–20.

9. See Pajares, M. F. "Teachers' Beliefs and Educational Research: Cleaning Up a Messy Construct." *Review of Educational Research*, 1992, *62*(3), 307–322.

10. Darling-Hammond, L., Berry, B. T., Haselkorn, D., and Fideler, E. "Teacher Recruitment, Selection, and Induction: Policy Influences on the Supply and Quality of Teachers." In L. Darling-Hammond and G. Sykes (eds.), *Teaching as the Learning Profession: Handbook of Policy and Practice* (pp. 183–232). San Francisco: Jossey-Bass, 1999.

11. Darling-Hammond and others, 1999, pp. 183–232.

12. The school name is a pseudonym.

13. My colleagues include the elementary education program faculty at the University of Wisconsin-Madison. The colleagues who codirected this work are Mary Louise Gomez and Kenneth Zeichner.

14. There is a description of the program in Ladson-Billings, G. "Preparing Teachers for Diversity: Historical Perspectives, Current Trends, and Future Directions." In L. Darling-Hammond and G. Sykes (eds.), *Teaching as the Learning Profession: Handbook of Policy and Practice* (pp. 86–123). San Francisco: Jossey-Bass, 1999.

15. Wilson, S. "The Secret Garden of Teacher Education. *Phi Delta Kappan*, 1990, *72*, 204–209.

16. Schwab, J. "The Practical: Arts of Eclectic." *School Review*, 1971, *79*(4), 493–542.

17. Schwab, 1971, pp. 494, 496.

18. Kaplan, D., and Manners, R. *Culture Theory*. Englewood Cliffs, N.J.: Prentice Hall, 1972, p. 11.

19. Kaplan and Manners, 1972, p. 11.

20. Shulman, L. "Knowledge and Teaching: Foundations of the New Reform." *Harvard Educational Review*, 1987, *57*, 1–22.

21. Shulman, 1987, p. 9.

22. Holmes Group Report. *Teachers for Tomorrow's Schools*. East Lansing, Mich: Holmes Group Report, 1986; Johnston, J., Spalding, J., Paden, R., and Ziffren, A. *Those Who Can: Undergraduate Programs to Prepare Arts and Sciences Majors for Teaching*. Washington, D.C.: American Association of Colleges of Teacher Education, 1989.

23. Shulman, 1987, p. 8.

24. Grossman, P. *The Making of a Teacher: Teacher Knowledge and Teacher Education*. New York: Teachers College Press, 1990.

25. Shulman, 1987, pp. 9–10.

26. Grossman, 1990, pp. 7–8.

27. Giroux, H., and Simon, R. "Popular Culture and Critical Pedagogy: Everyday Life as a Basis for Curriculum Knowledge." In H. Giroux and P. McLaren (eds.), *Critical Pedagogy, the State and Cultural Struggle* (pp. 236–92). Albany, N.Y.: SUNY Press, 1989.

28. Giroux and Simon, 1989, p. 239.

29. Giroux and Simon, 1989, p. 237.

30. This comment came out as a result of a program review where external reviewers had the opportunity to talk with a cross-section of our students.

31. Zeichner, K. *Teacher Education for Social Responsibility*. Paper presented at the annual meeting of the American Educational Research Association, Chicago, 1991.

32. Ladson-Billings, G. *The Dreamkeepers: Successful Teachers of African American Children*. San Francisco: Jossey-Bass, 1994.

Chapter Two

1. See, for example, King, J. "'Thank You for Opening Our Mind:' On Praxis, Transmutation, and Black Studies in Teacher Development." In J. King, E. Hollins, and W. Hayman (eds.), *Preparing Teachers for Cultural Diversity* (pp. 156–169). New York: Teachers College Press, 1997; Irvine, J. J. "Making Teacher Education Culturally Responsive." In M. Dilworth (ed.), *Diversity in Teacher Education*. San Francisco: Jossey-Bass, 1992; Cochran-Smith, M. "Color Blindness and Basket Making Are Not the Answers: Confronting the Dilemmas of Race, Culture, and Language Diversity in Teacher Education." *American Educational Research Journal*, 1995, *32*, 493–522.
2. Haberman, M. *Star Teachers of Children in Poverty*. West Lafayette, Ind.: Kappa Delta Pi, 1995.

Chapter Three

1. Shujaa, M. (ed.). *Too Much Schooling, Too Little Education: A Paradox of Black Life in White Societies*. Trenton, N.J.: African World Press, 1994.
2. Cremin, L. *The Transformation of the School: Progressivism in American Education, 1876–1957*. New York: Vintage Books, 1961.
3. In the late 1960s and early 1970s teachers were encouraged to help their students participate in a process called valuing and values clarification. In the early 1990s a California legislator (John Vasconcellas) insisted that California students needed instruction to raise their "self-esteem." This self-esteem effort became the subject of the nationally syndicated comic strip, "Doonesbury."

4. Cartwright, M. (with D'Orso, M.). *For the Children: Lessons from a Visionary Principal.* New York: Doubleday, 1993.

5. See the vivid examples in the video, *Children in America's Schools with Bill Moyers,* produced by Jeffrey Hayden and Kelley Cauthen, South Carolina Educational Television, 1996. To purchase a VHS copy call SCETV Marketing Department, 1-800-553-7752 or e-mail [parker@scetv.org].

6. See Anderson, J. *The Education of Blacks in the South, 1860–1935.* Chapel Hill, N.C.: University of North Carolina Press, 1988; Siddle-Walker, V. *Their Highest Potential: An African American Community in the Segregated South.* Chapel Hill, N.C.: University Of North Carolina Press, 1996; Garcia, E. "Educating Mexican American Students: Past Treatment and Recent Developments in Theory, Research, Policy, and Practice." In J. A. Banks and C. M. Banks (eds.), *Handbook of Research on Multicultural Education* (pp. 372–387). New York: Macmillan, 1995; Lee, S. *Unraveling the "Model Minority" Stereotype: Listening to Asian American Youth.* New York: Teachers College Press, 1996.

7. Fordham, S., and Ogbu, J. "Black Students' School Success: Coping with the Burden of 'Acting White.'" *Urban Review,* 1986, *18*(1), 176–206.

8. See *USA Today,* "Black White Income Differences," July 25, 2000.

9. From her "Statement of Purpose," a document that each cohort member submitted as a part of his or her application to the program.

10. Freire, P. *Pedagogy of the Oppressed.* New York: Seabury Press, 1968.

11. The cooperating teacher later published a wonderful paper about teaching this unit. In order not to compromise the school's, teachers', and students' anonymity I have chosen not to cite that article.

12. Williams, K. *Gallimoto.* New York: Lothrop Lee & Shephard, 1990.

13. Rist, R. "Student Social Class and Teacher Expectations: The Self-Fulfilling Prophecy in Ghetto Education." *Harvard Educational Review*, 1970, *40*, 411–451.

14. Ladson-Billings, G., and Gomez, M. L. "Just Showing Up: Supporting Early Literacy Through Teachers' Professional Communities." *Phi Delta Kappan*, in press.

15. Shulman, L. "Knowledge and Teaching: Foundations of the New Reform." *Harvard Educational Review*, 1987, *57*, 1–22.

Chapter Four

1. Taken from Gates, H. L., and McKay, N. (eds.). *The Norton Anthology of African American Literature*. New York: Norton, 1997, p. 1591.

2. Ladson-Billings, G. "Towards a Theory of Cultural Pedagogy." *American Educational Research Journal*, 1995, *32*, 465–492.

3. Gordon, B. "The Marginalized Discourse of Minority Intellectual Thought." In C. Grant (ed.), *Research and Multicultural Education: From Margins to the Mainstream* (pp. 19–31). London: Falmer Press, 1991.

4. Kunjufu, J. *Developing Discipline and Positive Self Images in Black Children*. Chicago: African American Images, 1984.

5. *Up-talk* is a term for the linguistic style of white suburban teenagers. It is distinctive in its use of an inflection on the end of all sentences. The speaker always seems to be asking a question, even when making a statement such as, "It's a sunny day?"

6. Tatum, B. D. *Why Are All the Black Kids Sitting Together in the Cafeteria and Other Conversations About Race*. New York: Basic Books, 1997.

7. See, for example, the discussion of Martin Luther King Jr.'s image in Dyson, M. E., *I May Not Get There With You: The True Martin Luther King, Jr*. New York: Free Press, 1999.

8. McIntosh, P. "White Privilege: Unpacking the Invisible Knapsack." *Independent School*, Winter 1990, 31–36.

9. See Allen, T. *The Invention of the White Race:* Vol. 1: *Racial Oppression and Social Control.* London: Verso Press, 1994.

10. Tatum, 1997.

Chapter Five

1. Baldwin, J. "A Talk to Teachers." In R. Simonson and S. Walker, *The Graywolf Annual Five: Multicultural Literacy: Opening the American Mind.* St. Paul, Minn.: Graywolf Press, 1988, p. 4.

2. See Morris, A. *The Origins of the Civil Rights Movement: Black Communities Organizing for Change.* New York: Free Press, 1984.

3. Clark, S. (with Brown, C.). *Ready from Within: Septima Clark and the Civil Rights Movement.* Navarro, Calif.: Wild Trees Press, 1986; Horton, M. (with Kohl, J., and Kohl, H.). *The Long Haul: An Autobiography.* New York: Doubleday, 1986.

4. Mills, K. *This Little Light of Mine: The Life of Fannie Lou Hamer.* New York: Dutton, 1993.

5. Aaronsohn, L. "Learning to Teach for Empowerment." *Radical Teacher,* 1992, 40, 44–46.

6. Harding, V. *Hope and History: Why We Must Share the Story of the Movement.* Maryknoll, N.Y.: Orbis Press, 1990.

7. Tate, W. "Race, Retrenchment, and the Reform of School Mathematics." *Phi Delta Kappan,* 1994, 76, 477–484.

8. Torres-Guzman, M. "Stories of Hope in the Midst of Despair: Culturally Responsive Education for Latino Students in an Alternative High School in New York City." Paper presented at the 10th Anniversary Colloquium of the College Board's Council on Academic Affairs. New York, May 4–5, 1989.

9. See, for example, Wade, R. (ed.). *Community Service Learning: A Guide to Including Service in the Public School Curriculum.* Albany, N.Y.: SUNY Press, 1997.

10. I have used an anglicized pseudonym for this boy because his real name is anglicized.

11. I have chosen not to cite the cohort members' master's papers because it would reveal their identities. However, they did give me informed written consent to quote from them.

12. Delpit, L. "The Silenced Dialogue: Power and Pedagogy in Educating Other People's Children." *Harvard Educational Review*, 1988, 58, 280–298.

13. Herrnstein, R., and Murray, C. *The Bell Curve: Intelligence and Class Structure in American Life*. New York: Free Press, 1994.

14. Baker, B. "'Childhood' in the Emergence and Spread of U.S. Public Schools." Unpublished master's thesis, Department of Curriculum and Instruction, University of Wisconsin-Madison, 1995.

15. Hilliard, A. "Do We Have the Will to Educate All the Children?" *Educational Leadership*, Sept. 1991, 36.

16. Morse, J. "Sticking to the Script." *Time*, Mar. 6, 2000, pp. 60–61.

Chapter Six

1. See Dyson, M. E. *I May Not Get There with You: The True Martin Luther King, Jr.* New York: Free Press, 2000.

2. National Commission for Teaching and America's Future. *What Matter's Most? Teaching and America's Future*. New York: National Commission for Teaching and America's Future, 1996.

3. Haberman, M. "The Pedagogy of Poverty vs. Good Teaching." *Phi Delta Kappan*, 1991, 73(4), 290–294.

4. Bransford, J., Brown, A., and Cocking, R. *How People Learn: Brain, Mind, Experience and School*. Washington, D.C.: National Academy Press, 1999.

Appendix A: Methodology

1. See Ladson-Billings, G. "Toward a Theory of Culturally Relevant Pedagogy." *American Educational Research Journal*, 1995, 35, 465–491.

2. See Spradley, J. *The Ethnographic Interview*. New York: Holt, Rinehart and Winston, 1979.
3. George Spindler is known as the father of educational anthropology. He and his wife, Louise, have edited a series of ethnographies (published by Holt, Rinehart and Winston) that demonstrate the intense and intimate relationships researchers develop with participants and communities.
4. I began the data analysis using NU*DIST but enrolled in an NVIVO course half-way through the project. I later re-entered the data in the NVIVO program. Both software programs are published by Sage Publications.
5. Brenda decided to return home to look for work. Her home community was less diverse than her preparation-year school.

Appendix B: The Teach for Diversity Program

1. This section is adapted from the "Teach for Diversity" brochure that Mary Louise Gomez and I developed. These brochures were distributed throughout the Midwest, to historically black colleges, and on our own campus career planning and placement office.
2. CGI is a theory of early mathematics learning developed by Thomas Carpenter and Elizabeth Fennema. Conceptual change theory is a science education theory developed by Peter Hewson. These theorists are University of Wisconsin-Madison scholars.

Index